Our Crowded Planet

Our Crowded Planet:

Essays on the Pressures of Population

FAIRFIELD OSBORN, EDITOR

Sponsored by
The Conservation Foundation

Doubleday & Company, Inc.
Garden City, New York
1962

Introduction

FAIRFIELD OSBORN

This book stems from the conviction that the inordinately rapid increase of populations in this world is the most essential problem that faces *everybody everywhere*. Slowly, all too slowly, we are learning that the pervasive and complex effects of ever increasing numbers of people are almost invariably harmful. The results of population pressures are not merely physical, such as the daily crisis of starvation facing hundreds of millions of people; they generate as well a host of other undesirable conditions in human life affecting not only the happiness and conduct of the individual but involving also basic questions of economics, religion, forms of government, and, finally, the ultimate dilemma of war or peace.

With these thoughts in mind, the gathering together of the material in this book seemed both timely and of large importance. To accomplish this, letters were written to a number of people of varied background and experience, inviting them to express their opinion on the population question as it related to their own special fields of interest.

7

Care was taken not to indicate what kind of a response would be welcome, for it would prove of little value to obtain views only from those who could be relied upon to concur with the conviction that population growth is indeed "the most essential problem." The invitation merely stated the premise "that the worldwide significance of steadily increasing population pressures on all phases of man's environment and future well-being is too little understood."

The attitudes of a number of the authors, it is true, were known a priori because they had, on more than one occasion, expressed themselves vigorously on the subject. However, the thoughts of others were not known, such as those who deal with the subjects of the Humanities, Mores, Peace, Nature, and Biological Principles, and, finally, questions pertaining to Religion.

We do indeed live in a fast-moving age. Merely a decade ago, relatively casual and limited attention was paid to population growth and its consequences. Nevertheless, a body of opinion has crystallized in recent years. Initially, this focused principally upon whether or not it would be possible to produce enough food and other essentials to meet the basic needs of oncoming additional millions of human beings. Studies by international bodies were launched that concluded with the somber news that more than half the people on the earth were undernourished, many of them acutely so. Arguments followed as to the capacity of present-day science and technology to meet ever mounting demands, not only as to food production but as to other basic materials that today are considered necessary for a "decent standard of living." Latterly this measure of welfare has focused more and more upon the immense disparity between the so-called have and have-not peoples. Bridging the gap between these two groups of humanity has now rightly become one of the great issues of modern times.

In this transitional period of public opinion, there still are powerful influences, speaking either for the policies of various governments or in the defense of religious doctrine. These are not prepared either to acknowledge or deal with the situation, failing to recognize that ever increasing numbers of people, of whatever nation or religion, only serve to magnify problems that are already so acute and so universal. There still remain, also, marginal bodies of opinion that decry the idea that "the population explosion" need be looked upon as a critical matter for the reason that anticipated developments in science and technology can be relied upon to meet any future demands for food supplies or other material needs. It is hoped that one of the values of this book will be to show that the consequences of population growth reach far beyond the question of physical want, primary in importance as it is.

The position of the Roman Catholic Church, because of its influence in many countries and among many peoples, has been a major deterrent to coordinated action to deal with the problem. The Church's position rests principally upon the grounds that some of the evidently most practical and effective measures of limiting population growth would be unacceptable within the Church's doctrine and contravene the "natural law."

The enigma presented by the Roman Catholic position is its lack of recognition that mankind has already accepted the benefits of medical science that have brought about "death control" which are totally *unnatural*. These benefits have to a major degree eliminated the normal processes of nature that until recent times were the principal factors that kept the birth rate and death rate in balance. The classic Roman axiom of "quid pro quo" is still valid.

At a time when so much attention is engrossed by the miracles of science and technology, we are hesitant, indeed often unwilling, to think of man as subject to such seemingly remote influences as "biological principles." In the era of the "machine age," in an era of vast cities created and operated by the extraordinary ingenuity of modern technical skills, in an era when man has orbited the earth and is reaching toward the mysteries of other planets and outer space, one can easily be deluded into believing that man has finally liberated himself from the compulsions of the so-called "laws of nature" that have heretofore controlled all forms of life on this earth. Of these laws none is more evident or universal than that which demonstrates that too great numbers of any given species, whether of man or other form of life, inevitably result in a climax problem that must, in one manner or another, be resolved.

Man, it is true, is unique in his powers. As observed in the concluding essay, "Man is now, whether he likes it or not, and indeed whether he knows it or not . . . the sole agent for the evolutionary process on earth. He is responsible for the future of this planet."

Included in these powers is the capacity to make decisions concerning the future. Man may allow himself to suffer atomic devastation or to face ever mounting difficulties due to pressures of his own numbers. In either eventuality, the choice is his. Both choices, different as they seem to be, are approximately of the same magnitude.

The views expressed in this book are compositely similar to a prism, throwing different light-values upon this present dramatic period in human affairs. Life requires no less than vision and no more than action.

CONTENTS

FAIRFIELD OSBORN   Introduction   7

PART I

Population Pressures on Man's Natural Environment

MARSTON BATES   Man as a Member of a Biological Community   19

CHARLES G. DARWIN   The Law of Population Increase   29

PAUL B. SEARS   The American Environment   37

FREDERICK H. OSBORN   Overpopulation and Genetic Selection   51

FRANK FRASER DARLING   The Population Explosion and the Natural Environment   71

13

PART II

Population Pressures on Economic and Political Trends

EUGENE R. BLACK	Population Increase and Economic Development	83
EARLE L. RAUBER	Industrial Growth in the Twentieth Century	93
LORD BOYD ORR	Mankind's Supply of Food	103
SOLLY ZUCKERMAN	Environmental Planning for an Increased Population	109
HENRY STEELE COMMAGER	Overpopulation and the New Nations	117
GRENVILLE CLARK	Population Pressures and Peace	123
ARNOLD J. TOYNBEE	The Menace of Overpopulation	135

PART III

Population Pressures in Specific Areas

WALTER C. LOWDERMILK	The Promise of Agriculture in the Less Developed Lands	145
M. C. CHAGLA	India's Dilemma	159

CONTENTS

CHIKAO HONDA   Japan's Solution   165

ENRIQUE BELTRAN   Latin America's Prospects   175

PART IV

The Population Problem and Religion

THE REV. ROBERT I.
GANNON   A Roman Catholic Speaks   187

THE RT. REV. JAMES
A. PIKE   A Protestant's View   197

PART V

Population Pressures on Morals and Ethics

JOSEPH WOOD   A Naturalist Looks at
KRUTCH   Overpopulation   207

ANDRÉ MAUROIS   The Good Life   215

JULIAN HUXLEY   Too Many People!   223

Selected List of Readings   235

PART I

Population Pressures on Man's Natural Environment

Man as a Member of
a Biological Community

MARSTON BATES

Throughout nature there is a balance between the reproductive rate of a given species of organism and the hazards of existence for that species. Elephants produce few young, while the spawn of oysters is innumerable. It is, to be sure, a teetering balance, so that there are often shifts in abundance from year to year or generation to generation. It is generally true, however, that biological systems have a great deal of "play" or flexibility. If the hazards of existence continue for any length of time to be greater than can be met by the reproductive rate, the species is started on the road to extinction. If reproduction exceeds mortality for any long period, the result is some sort of catastrophe—sometimes taking the form of mass suicide, as with locusts or lemmings.

We are all aware that individual organisms—men, dogs, or oak trees—are made up of integrated systems of many different parts that, through balanced interaction, keep the individual alive and functioning. Physiologists use for this the elegant term "homeostasis." The biological community is also an integrated system, analogous to the individual in many ways, but the physiology of the community is less obvious, less well understood. The individuals in the community are like the cells in an organism; they are, similarly, of many different kinds, with different functions.

The community is held together, basically, by food relations. We have the producers, the green plants, that build up the chemical energy of organic compounds using the radiant energy of sunlight. These plants are eaten by the first-order consumers, the "key industry animals," which in turn become food in a variety of ways for the higher order consumers. In the end, the complex chemicals are reduced to simpler materials again by the decomposers—mostly microbes—ready to be used again by the green plants in the unending cycles of energy and materials in the system.

The human animal evolved as a part of this biological system. The protohominids or pre-men, and the early men—we can avoid the nice problem of where to draw the line between man and not-man—were primarily hunters, predators, second- or third-order consumers. We have evidence of this from the animal bones found associated with the South African australopithecines and other fossil sites. Further, man can digest a wide variety of kinds of raw meat, from oysters and insects to fish and beef; while his possible vegetable diet, without cooking, is limited. He thus could not have become predominantly vegetarian until he had learned to control fire, though he probably always gathered such digestible plant products as fruits and nuts.

We can know nothing about the birth rates or the sexual habits of the various species of manlike fossils, though we can make more or less plausible guesses. We can assume that through most of the Pleistocene or Ice Age the different hominids conformed to the general rule that birth and death must be in long-term balance. In the long run, it appears that mortality exceeded natality for all species except those in the evolutionary line of modern man, because all of the other hominids became extinct. The causes of death are necessarily obscure. There is evidence, from the australopithecines, from Peking man, from Neanderthal and other remains, that hominids early started the curious behavior pattern of killing each other. On the other hand, Lewis Mumford's argument (in *The City in History*) that mass mutual slaughter, as in war, is a late development, a product of city formation and civilization, seems convincing. We simply have no way of evaluating the relative importance of homicide, disease, predation by big cats and crocodiles, and accidental hazards. Something, however, controlled population growth, because a hunting animal could not become very numerous within the limits of the food supply.

Modern man's reproductive rate is about the lowest of that of any mammal, though the rate for elephants is even lower. This can be regarded as co-adaptive with his relatively low death rate during the period when his biological characteristics were being shaped by the processes of organic evolution. The fecundity—the reproductive potential—of prehuman species and early men may have been even lower than that of modern man. Mothers, among existing hunting peoples, nurse their young for at least two years; and with a nomadic hunting life, prolonged nursing would seem necessary. With contemporary human females, ovulation during lactation is quite irregular, though it occurs, and in many cultures there is a taboo on sexual intercourse as long as a child is being nursed. It is very possible that with early men, ovulation was physiologically suppressed during lactation, which would result in an automatic wide spacing of offspring. Certainly a hunting mother, often on the move, would hardly be able to take care simultaneously of several dependent infants.

Infant mortality is very high in many contemporary societies; and there is a relatively high mortality among the young in all animal species. Infant mortality with Stone Age man, however, may have been much lower than in the crowded agricultural societies we know. Much of this mortality is due to diarrheas, caused by infections maintained under crowded conditions and aggravated by premature weaning.

Whatever the details, the populations of hominids must have been rather stable and sparse over long periods of time in the Pleistocene. This changed suddenly (in a geological sense) with the Neolithic development of agriculture. Between ten and fifteen thousand years ago the human species started on a spree of population growth that has no known parallel. This growth was probably the consequence both of increased birth rates and decreased death rates under settled conditions of assured food supply. The growth in numbers was irregular and slow over most of this period, up to the spectacular spurt of the last hundred years or so.

Post-Neolithic man, with the development of agriculture and a whole series of other technologies, has been able to escape the biological controls that ordinarily work to maintain balance within the community. The late Alan Gregg, of the medical division of the Rockefeller Foundation, compared this human growth with the wild growth of cancer cells within an individual organism. The analogy has frightening parallels. It can be argued that man at the moment is doing all right (though I think few people are really happy about the present human condition). But if you could ask individual cancer cells growing in an organism, they would probably also think they were doing fine, not caring and not realizing that in their wild growth they were destroying the organism and thus inevitably also destroying themselves.

Argument by analogy can be very misleading, and the present organism-community comparison is at most suggestive. Yet the problem of balance remains. The present rate of human population growth obviously cannot be maintained. With additions to the world's people every month equivalent in numbers to the inhabitants of the city of Chicago, there will be standing room only in no time at all. And even if we learn to live happily on soup made from algae, there remain many kinds of problems dealt with by the various authors in this book.

Population size and rate of change are necessarily consequences of the relation between births and deaths. In ecological language, it is said that the numbers of any particular species are the result of the interaction of the "biotic potential" and the "environmental resistance." When we start to look at the human situation in these ecological terms, we at once find ourselves involved with factors quite different from those operating in other animal populations—the factors that turn on human culture. The post-Neolithic increase in numbers of men is a consequence, not so much of biological evolution as of cultural development, especially of agriculture, medicine, and technology in general.

There are many parallels between biological evolution and cultural development. In both we find progressive change tending toward ever better adaptation (but with changes also sometimes apparently maladaptive); we find geographical differentiation, diffusion or spread, hybridization or blending, and the like. There are also basic differences. The means of innovation in culture is invention or discovery; in biological evolution, mutation. The mode of transmission in the one is through teaching and learning, through symbol systems like language; in the other, through genetic heredity. The rate of change in cultural traits can be very fast, compared with change through biological evolution. Human biology, as far as we can tell, has not altered since the days when Cro-Magnon man painted those powerful figures on the walls of caves in southern Europe; but the culture, the behavior, the way of life of this human animal today can hardly be compared with that in the Stone Age, so greatly has it altered.

Cultural and biological factors interact to control birth and death, whether in Cro-Magnon or in modern man. Ovulation is biological; age at marriage, ways of getting a wife, even details of copulation, are under cultural control. Death in the long run is biological, but it has been postponed for the individual by cultural innovations, through assured food supply and through medical practices. The postponement of death has been achieved in large measure deliberately, through the development of science and the spread of scientific information. Isn't it logical, then, to devote equal attention to the birth side of the equation?

24

And is contraception any more "unnatural" than vaccination? We have, to be sure, modified birth rates to some extent, but the bulk of our attention has been given to mortality, with consequences that are beginning to worry everyone.

I started with a comparison between the organism and the biotic community. Curiously, we know a great deal more about the functioning of the organism, about physiology, than we do about the functioning of the community, about ecology. But this latter study is getting more and more attention, and our understanding of the interrelations among organisms is steadily increasing. One principle that is beginning to emerge from both field and laboratory investigations is that the more complex the community, the more stable the component populations. Animal numbers in the arctic tundra, where there are comparatively few species, fluctuate greatly over the years, while populations in the complex tropical rain forest remain remarkably constant. The simpler situation is more liable to catastrophe because there are fewer possibilities for adjustment within the system if anything happens to one of its component parts.

All of the operations of modern man are directed toward the simplification of the community. Man, over much of the land surface of the world, is quite successfully becoming an ecological dominant. Vegetation that he does not want is replaced by crops he can use. The crops for the most part are vast stands of single plant species. Man has become vegetarian, a first-order consumer, with the aid of fire for cooking. He still likes meat, and for this he moves into the position of a second-order consumer, raising fodder for his cattle or grain for his swine. Furthermore, he will not tolerate plants (weeds) that compete for his crops, or parasites or predators that compete for his domesticated animals. He has also made himself terminal in the food system: he long ago ceased to be a significant food supply for lions or crocodiles, and he has lately learned more and more about how to defeat mosquitoes, fleas, intestinal worms, bacteria, and other parasites. He even tries to eliminate himself from the decomposer system by means of lead-lined caskets.

Now all of this is very efficient. There is a great loss of energy between each step in food interchange in the biological community, so that second-order consumers are necessarily rarer than first-order, third than second, and so on. The vast numbers of Homo sapiens could only be supported as first- or second-order consumers. But this simplified man-centered system is only maintained by constant vigilance. The fields of uniform crops are fine for man, but they also afford new opportunities for all kinds of possible pests. We defeat the pests with an insecticide, but the pests presently develop resistance, and a new insecticide must be found. This is happening now with bacteria and antibiotics, and many physicians are greatly worried because a powerful tool is deteriorating through failure to recognize ecological and biological principles. Man constantly encounters unexpected effects in his remaking of nature. Predators are controlled and rodents become a pest. Elm trees are sprayed with DDT to kill the beetles associated with Dutch elm disease, and next year robins are killed by eating the earthworms that have eaten the dead elm leaves. And so it goes: efficient, yes, but also precarious.

No one, certainly, would advocate going back to the

"natural" state of the Stone Age, but, equally, no one can view the brave new world toward which we are heading with much enthusiasm. Francis Bacon long ago observed that "we cannot command nature without obeying her" and in the arrogance of our present success in command, we forget that obedience may also be required for survival. As Charles Elton has remarked, "Unless one merely thinks man was intended to be an all-conquering and sterilizing power in the world, there must be some general basis for understanding what it is best to do. This means looking for some wise principle of coexistence between man and nature, even if it be a modified kind of man and a modified kind of nature." And one necessary modification of man, surely, is some curbing, some balance, some intelligent adaptation, of his present cancer-like spree of reproduction.

SIR CHARLES G. DARWIN, the British physicist (grandson of biologist Charles Darwin), was educated at Trinity College, Cambridge. He has been a lecturer in physics at Manchester University and a lecturer in mathematics at Christ's College, Cambridge. From 1923 to 1936 he was Tait Professor of Natural Philosophy at Edinburgh University and then Master of Christ's College, Cambridge. In 1938 he became director of the National Physical Laboratory, a post he held until 1949. Sir Charles is an honorary fellow of Christ's and Trinity Colleges, Cambridge, and in 1935 received the Royal Medal of the Royal Society. In addition to various papers in theoretical physics he is the author of two books, *The New Conceptions of Matter* and *The Next Million Years*.

The Law of Population Increase

CHARLES G. DARWIN

It is curious how long the world is taking to perceive that we are living in what is a fantastically abnormal period of history, and one which must inevitably end soon. The first warning note was given by Malthus in 1799, but his forecast of disaster was defeated by the invention of railways, steamships and such things only a little later, and too few people noticed that in half of his forecast he was perfectly right, for the population of England did double itself in fifty years twice over during the succeeding century. Again, in Chapter III of *The Origin of Species*, there is written: "Even slow-breeding man has doubled in twenty-five years, and at this rate, in a few thousand years, there would literally not be standing room for his progeny" —and it may be noted that this is very much of an understatement, for, with the high figure of increase he takes, the condition of standing room only would be reached in about five hundred years. It is these increases, already noted more than a century ago, that make the present time so abnormal. It had taken the world nearly two thousand years for its numbers to be doubled between about A.D. 1 and A.D. 1750, but then in the next two centuries it has been multiplied by five, and the demographers tell us that the rate of increase is still itself increasing.

If we could accept the present conditions as a normal state of the world, that would imply that this steady increasing is also a normal state. We have nearly three billion people now: therefore by the year 2000 we shall have more than five billion, by 2050 ten billion, by 2100 twenty billion, and by 2150 forty billion. It is quite evident that the world, already crowded in many parts, would by then be most impossibly overcrowded. We can say with confidence that all our present conditions of life cannot continue for two more centuries, and this is most likely a great overestimate. We have—within what the historians would call an exceedingly short period—to revert to a mode of life which in one way or another will keep the numbers of the human race roughly constant.

The students of population are naturally concerned over these questions, but chiefly for a shorter range of time than this. The matter resolves itself into what may be called the Malthusian balance, on the one hand how many people there will be, and on the other how they will live. On the one side the increase is nearly fifty million a year, and catastrophes such as famines or wars—even atomic war—cannot make any serious inroad on the increase during the next fifty years. Nor is it to be expected that such humane methods of reduction as contraception can extend fast enough during that time to make much difference. It may be granted that they are spreading fast, but it seems most improbable that such practices should be used by something like a billion people before the end of the present generation, and anything less than this would be insignificant. We have got to accept that there will be well over five billion people fifty years hence.

On the other side of the balance, the agriculturalists assure us that it should be possible to double the world's food production within the fifty years. It will call for a lot of capital for equipment and for irrigation, but it will also call for a radical revision in methods of farming by hundreds of millions of farmers, and this means a social upset in most of the world that seems unlikely to be achieved in what is hardly more than a single generation. There are also the problems of providing the equipment of metals, etc., that are essential for civilized life. The more these latter questions are considered the more formidable they are seen to be, but our technologists do know how to find substitute materials in many cases, so that the difficulties may not be quite so basic as is the provision of food. The central problem would appear to be food.

When we recollect that more than half the world is undernourished even now, it is impossible to be happy about this. In the conference held in Rome in 1954, reference was made to the previous seven years, in which agriculture had achieved the triumphant success of putting up food production by 8 percent. But during those seven years the world had increased in numbers by 11 percent, so that we were hungrier at the end in spite of these triumphs. Does this not mean that fifty years hence it is all too likely that there will be twice as many hungry people as there are now, well over three billion of them?

We have tended to look at the subject, by first considering how many people there will be, and then considering how they are to be fed. It is the natural way of reckoning the balance, especially since we do know the way to go about producing more food, even if we are not always very successful in doing it. But it is well worth looking at the subject the other way about. First ask the question how much food can we hope to produce fifty years hence, and then no matter what it may be, will there not surely be far too many mouths asking for it?

This thought is suggested by the consideration that man is an animal, and broadly speaking he obeys the laws of zoology. One of the most universal of these laws may be called the law of increase, that every generation of every animal always produces some excess in the next generation, which is then cut down again roughly to constancy by the operations of natural selection. Whenever an animal is turned loose in a new area, as for example when rats from a shipwreck escape into an uninhabited island, they immediately start to multiply in numbers, until there are so many of them that they exhaust the food supply. In the billion years or so since his ancestors first came into existence man has obeyed this law, and he is most emphatically obeying it just now. Through the great discoveries of the scientific revolution we have found how any given piece of land can support ten, or perhaps even twenty times as many human beings as it could before. We have responded just as the rats do, with only the difference that they have a new generation every year, whereas we take thirty years for it. Slow-breeding man is still illustrating the law of increase even after two hundred years, but it is evident that he cannot continue to do so for a great deal longer, no matter how successful we may be in increasing the other side of the Malthusian balance. If we should succeed in still further increasing the food supply, the effect might be to allow us to increase our numbers thirtyfold instead of twentyfold, but this would merely mean that the law of increase could continue to operate as it is doing now for an extra fifty years or so.

It is worth conjecturing what will happen if the law of increase continues to be allowed to work uncontrolledly as it does now. We shall quite soon reach a limit when life becomes hard again in the manner that it did only a few centuries ago. This will end such things as affluent societies and welfare states, because only a limited fraction of those born can expect to survive for what we now consider the normal expectation of life. This should not mean a relapse into barbarism, for the very simple reason that barbarians can only live at a much lower density of numbers than civilized people, and so the retention of civilization will have a strong survival value. But it is hardly to be expected that this civilization will carry with it the kindly, rather facile charitableness that we tend to associate with it. It must become much tougher, and our descendants will look back to the nineteenth and twentieth centuries as a golden age of easy life.

It is then worth considering whether there is any possibility of avoiding these increases and what that would entail. In the first place, if we can find a way of controlling our numbers, why do we not put it into practice at once: it is not evident that a world of five billion is in any way better than a world of three billion. To do this we have to find a way of breaking a law which all our ancestors have obeyed for a billion years, and it is evidently a most formidable thing to attempt. It might indeed be judged hopeless, if it were not for the fact that there is another universal genetic law which we still obey, though we have

33

found out how to get round its consequences. This is known as the law of the noninheritance of acquired characters. Among animals each individual acquires all its characters from its germ cell, and none from any of the characters its parents have acquired during their lives. Genetically we still obey this law completely, but we have got round its consequences by our ability to communicate with our fellows. For example, our present explosive increase of numbers is due originally to only a few individuals, the scientists who inaugurated and developed the scientific revolution, and yet the whole human race has enjoyed the consequent prosperity. Can we hope to break the law of increase in some similar manner?

There is one most formidable genetic consequence to be faced if this aim is achieved. For the past two centuries we have succeeded in some countries in avoiding the main consequences of natural selection: anyone can survive without having to undergo the stringent test of the struggle for life. Our aim would be to extend this condition to the whole world. It may do little harm for a few generations, but it is questionable whether it will not carry the consequence of a gradual degeneration in human qualities in the long run through the preservation of all the inferior mutations in man's genetic equipment. Such mutations are constantly occurring in the case of man as well as of all animals, and in the past it has been through their perpetual elimination in the stringent struggle for life that the marvels of evolution have occurred. If then we succeed in our aim of limiting numbers artificially, have we got to face a slow degeneration in the qualities of the human race?

More serious difficulties arise when the machinery of

limitation is considered. There would be an instability in the process in that if half the world accepted limitation, while the other half refused, all too soon the limiters would be in a minority, and in the end the nonlimiters would dominate the world. To have any hope of success then there would have to be a worldwide enforcement. This would at once attack one of the predominating characteristics of mankind, our hatred of discipline, which we are apt to sanctify by calling it the love of freedom. It would seem then that success is only likely to be achieved at the expense of a sacrifice of one of our most prized ideals. And there remains the question how any world government could be established which would be capable of enforcing such a system in perpetuity.

I have tried to set out some of the problems to be faced if we are to achieve a continuation of human living in the manner that we would most certainly wish for. In every way let us strive to accomplish this, but the prospects do not seem to be very good, and as a personal opinion it seems to me unlikely that we shall succeed in continuing our present conditions of life over any long period. To judge by many authors this would seem to be regarded as the end of any world worth thinking about, but I do not agree. From the writings of the past, when natural selection was in full operation, man appears to have been as happy as he is now, and I see no reason to think that in the future, when the struggle for life again becomes severe, the human race will lose happiness, even if they do look back with regret to the passing of the golden age in which we are now living.

PAUL B. SEARS, Professor Emeritus of Conservation at Yale University, is a noted biologist and ecologist. Most recently (1950) he established at Yale University the country's first graduate program of research and instruction in the conservation of natural resources. Dr. Sears has taught at Ohio State, University of Nebraska, the University of Oklahoma, and at Yale until his retirement in 1960. He received his B.A. from Wesleyan, his M.A. from Nebraska, and his PH.D. from Chicago. He was president of the American Association for the Advancement of Science in 1956. Dr. Sears has written many books, among them: *Deserts on the March, This Is Our World, Who Are These Americans,* and *Life And Environment.*

The American Environment

PAUL B. SEARS

The most obvious aspect of the population problem is its possible threat to individual survival. For this reason much of the "scientific" discussion has concerned itself with calculations as to how many people the earth in general and the United States in particular can be made to feed. There is perhaps the added reason that for all but about one percent of human time—and for many even today—the chief preoccupation of mankind has been to secure enough to eat.

Important as this approach may be, it can scarcely serve to arouse general interest on a continent whose resources north of Mexico have been substantially untouched until very recently and where technology is turning out food and other goods so abundantly that the bottleneck in industry is consumer enticement rather than production. Only by examining the more subtle aspects of the population problem can we hope to bring home to the people of the United States its urgency. If we assume any respect for the dignity of the individual it is not enough to talk of mere survival.

So let us advance the proposition that the individual must develop his self-interest within a pattern determined by the interplay of resources, population dynamics, and culture. This thought can be stated in various ways, using for example types of memoranda borrowed from mathematics. Thus Firey[1] has employed both symbolic logic and lattices, while I have found it convenient to discuss a simple formula (R/P) f (C), where R represents Resources, P Population, f the conventional function sign and C Culture.[2]

Using appropriate subscripts such as R_s for space, R_w for water, individual resources can be considered. Certainly it is clear that since resources are finite, they must be divisible among the existing population regardless of equity. It is also clear that the kinds and amounts of resources available affect cultural potential, while culture influences the kinds of resources made available, the efficiency with which they are used, and the prudence employed in their care. There is likewise a reciprocal relation between culture and population. Some cultures, especially the agrarian, esteem large families, others are more mindful of the need to provide favorable economic or other opportunities for the individual and less concerned with his future contribution to the family work force. The century-old constraint on family size among French peasantry represents an interesting balance between these two opposing tendencies.

Yet it should be noted that cultural emphasis on the importance of the individual has had a somewhat paradoxical effect, accounting in large part for the currently rapid increase in population in the United States and areas which it has tried to assist. For this emphasis affords the ethical justification in applying modern medicine and hygiene to decrease death rates and prolong the human life-span. Efforts along this line have far outstripped any compensating attempts to lower the birth rate.

Not only, then, do cultural sanctions affect the rate of population increase, but population pressures affect culture in significant ways. Here we refer to a physical principle of general application. Whenever dynamic particles are confined within a limited space, any increase in their number restricts freedom of action or in technical language decreases the mean free path and increases the degree of interference. This rule of experience rests solely upon the fact that the units are dynamic and applies equally to gas molecules in a stoppered liter flask, flies in a corked bottle, or people on an island.

Furthermore, if the energy in the system is in any way increased, as by heating the flask, adding oxygen to the bottle, or providing the islanders with automobiles that burn fossil fuel, the mean free path is further lessened. Since the introduction of the automobile the population of the United States has more than doubled, from about 75 million in 1900 to more than 160 million in 1960. Thus we have, after six decades, twice as many human beings moving about, say ten times faster than before on a conservative guess. Some measure of the effect on physical freedom may be had from the highway death toll of 37,000 in 1958[3] and perhaps a million injuries in the same length of time, the increasing restrictions on freedom of pedestrian movement and the growing burden of various types of regulatory legislation at all levels, to say nothing of taxes and the resultant inflation.

Against these liabilities must be weighed whatever advantages have come from greater mobility of goods and persons—a difficult if not impossible bit of accounting. More people see more places than before, but with less opportunity for deliberate appreciation, while traffic jams become steadily more serious, and the wear and tear on places worth seeing, such as Yosemite, is each year more evident.

Where resources are concerned, the liability column is heavily weighted. For example, more hydrocarbon fuel, iron and copper have been consumed since 1900 than in all previous history. This is due in large measure, though by no means solely, to the application of the internal combustion engine to transport. The construction of modern highways is an irreversible geological process that removes much land from any other type of use even in the long future, but here it is not yet possible to assess gain or loss. At best the present system of transporting increasing numbers of humans at increasing speeds is grossly inefficient. Traffic counts made in various places suggest that between 75 percent and 80 percent of the passenger automobiles, rated on the average at 100 horsepower (1 horsepower being rated at 10 manpower), are carrying single passengers. Save in wartime not even the grandest of monarchs could have been attended by a routine escort of 1000, yet the modern commoner thinks nothing of it on his daily ride.

I have been attempting to complete the justification for our simple memorandum by showing that as the functional relationship between resources and culture works both ways, so it is with culture and population. Not only do cultural standards affect family size and so the rate of population increase, but population increase definitely affects freedom within the culture. And in making this point I have felt obliged to introduce the effect of increasing amounts of nonrenewable energy within the system because it is a primary fact of modern life, in a very real sense stepping up the inevitable pressure that would occur solely from increasing numbers.

As with most biological processes, the relation between numbers and effectiveness (in this instance cultural plus biological) is not a simple and direct one. In human populations the initial phases of increase doubtless do promote the quality of the culture, since they permit specialization of activities and better organization. I think that the general record of development in innumerable communities is sufficient evidence of this, so we need not labor the point.

But we need not rely on general impression to convince us that after a community reaches a certain optimal size, which varies greatly of course with conditions, further increase is a liability instead of an asset. (See accompanying diagram.) To demonstrate this we need only refer to such studies as those of Spengler,[4] or to consult tax flow in some of the rapidly growing towns and cities of New England. Thus, just as we must consider available energy as a component of the population problem, we must also consider population distribution as well as absolute numbers.

This poses a particularly difficult problem in the United States, when the official guardians of community prosperity which we call chambers of commerce are obsessed with the idea that a community must enlarge to remain prosperous. Viewed simply as a biological phenomenon this confusion of growth with health is an error of the most serious kind, and we dare not lose sight of the fact

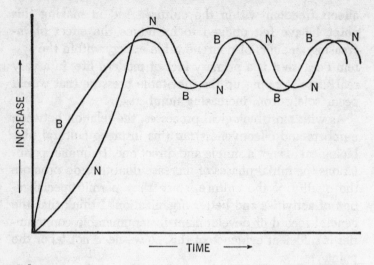

Schematic relation of population (N) to biological efficiency (B). For wild populations the initial increase of (B) with (N) is due to increased opportunities for breeding and spreading to range limits; later alternating pulsations at equilibrium level are based on field studies of population cycles. For man the initial phase is due to similar factors plus increased specialization and organization within cultures; the later phase represents operation of classical checks. This equilibrium level has been raised, first by the invention of agriculture, recently by scientific technology. Can it rise indefinitely?

that, whatever else they may be, man and his communities are basically biological phenomena.

Few men have had a better right to speak freely of the evils of unrestricted population growth than the late Dr. Alan Gregg. As a member of the Rockefeller Foundation he had devoted years to the compassionate relief of world health conditions. He certainly set full value on humanity.

Yet in a remarkable paper written shortly before his death he found only one biological analogue to present population dynamics—that of the unrestricted growth of cancer cells.[5] At the opposite pole, both ethically and intellectually we may place those who simply regard each new mouth as a new customer and measure the economic outlook in terms of the "baby crop."

Allowing ourselves the reasonable assumption that, barring cataclysm, food is not likely to be an important aspect of the North American population problem in the immediate future (yet making some mental reservations), what of the resource picture in general? Since volumes would be required for an adequate appraisal, only a few major points will be noted.

It is significant that two men who understood geology, Marsh[6] and Powell,[7] were among the first Americans to express concern over resource depletion, while our first textbook on the subject was written by the geologist Van Hise.[8] This, it seems to me, is because the geologist, unlike the modern economist, is trained to observe and think in the long perspective of time. Hence he is more concerned with the trend of process than with its rate. Such men saw through the fallacy entertained by many of the most intelligent of our early leaders, namely that the resources of this continent were literally inexhaustible, an error not apparent even to the discerning until the middle of the nineteenth century.

In fact, public concern was negligible until the first decade of the present century when interest, largely in forestry, was aroused by Theodore Roosevelt and Gifford Pinchot. This, plus the enlightened self-interest of large corporations intent on preserving supplies of raw material, has led to a vast improvement in American forestry and wood-processing. But on small private holdings, which comprise the bulk of our forest land, the level of management and processing lags, largely for economic reasons. Assuming as I do that the importance of wood will increase rather than diminish as time goes on, the potential exists if need arises, but could and should be enhanced by vigorous measures. We would benefit in more ways than one if unemployed were paid for timber-stand improvement instead of being compensated for idleness.

Public concern over soil loss and depletion did not begin until the series of misfortunes of the early 1930s but like forestry has borne visible fruit. However, the muddy rivers that prevail over much of the nation are proof that needless and costly loss continues. And since improvements in farm technology have reduced the acreage now necessary for that industry, any further reduction of soil loss will probably have to depend largely upon effective measures to purify stream flow. In the long view the indiscriminate appropriation of land, regardless of its fertility, for urban, industrial, and highway expansion will certainly affect our capacity to support an indefinitely growing population should that contingency arise. Estimates of land so alienated run to a million or more acres annually.[9]

The water situation is definitely not good, perhaps deteriorating in spite of growing concern. In a nation whose climates are as various as those of Norway, Russia, France, and Asia Minor and where population, thanks to ease of transport, is distributed largely without respect to inherent carrying capacity, water problems are many, complex, and far from uniform. Per capita use is increasing rapidly, while rivers double as sewers and domestic water sources.

Perhaps the most general comment that can be made is that we do not take care of the water we have in more humid areas, while the drier ones whose population has increased enormously continue to quarrel over the water that is available.

As to minerals, the progress of American industry has created a vortex that is drawing in the bulk of the world's production. It is encouraging to know that this is beginning to concern leaders in some of the industries whose attitude was long one of promoting public optimism.[10] Measures that are clearly indicated include more efficient production, priorities of importance in supplying the market, and adequate reclamation for reuse. Great strides in plastics research are fortunately being made, with consequent saving of metals.

The protection of wildlife receives increasing attention for a mixture of reasons, recreational, economic, aesthetic, and ethical. But it becomes more difficult, despite better techniques, as human numbers increase and occupy more space. Provision of suitable habitat is the key, a fact neglected until recently. Increasing numbers of private organizations are helping to shape public opinion and secure favorable governmental action where this is necessary. At best we must reconcile ourselves to the fact that anything like the one-time abundance and variety of wildlife is most unlikely.

This brief and inadequate glance at resources is enough to remind us that even in a nation as vast and varied as the United States the environment is finite. Quite properly this brings up a resource seldom mentioned as such, yet the one which subsumes all others—that is space. For it is the amount and quality of available space that in all biological observation sets limits to the indefinite multi-plication of any species. Yet there is widespread ignorance or even disbelief of the fact that this applies to man. We may dismiss on physiological grounds the suggestion that human beings are likely to colonize extraterrestrial space. More insistently held is the notion that technology will enable us to overcome the limitations of space we now live in and to take care of an indefinitely expanding population. This is an interesting case of a faith without metaphysics, whose validity must be judged, therefore, on the basis of its physical soundness before we consider its further im-plications.

The first hitch to be disposed of lies in the nature of technology. A scythe has its limitations, but it is much less subject to breakdown than a mowing machine. The source of any water supply may be affected by events in nature, but there are many more possibilities of interrupt-ing the flow of a 200-mile pipeline than of a good well or spring. Breakage or failure of a single element can stop a diesel locomotive or cut off the electrical current serving thousands. The more completely we depend upon tech-nology, the more intricate it must be. And the more elabo-rate a technological system, the more vulnerable it is, both the mechanical failure and human carelessness or inter-ference.

The second hitch to this dream of ceaseless breeding in a push-button paradise has already been mentioned. The biological rule of experience that no species has ever been observed to multiply indefinitely without coming into some kind of equilibrium with the limitations of its environment deserves as much respect as those biological principles we apply so confidently to the control of disease, improvement of domestic plants and animals, the growing of crops, and the care of the human body.

Vast as they are, the space and other resources of the United States are finite, hence potentially limiting. We can, of course, test those limits by the blind experiment of multiplying, meanwhile using science cleverly to postpone the ultimate consequence. Or we can choose to use science in a rational and humane fashion, appraising the limiting factors and controlling our numbers accordingly.

Meanwhile, as practical measures we can determine land-use potential and respect it, observe the economic fact that indefinite urban growth costs more than it returns, and be ever mindful that, beyond a certain point, the pressure of human numbers must compromise the freedom and dignity of the individual.

As compared with many older nations, the people of the United States still have a remarkable freedom of choice. Assuming we can avoid the tragedy that technological warfare could bring upon us, we have an opportunity to decide whether our concern is the quality of human existence or the mere business of survival.

REFERENCES

1. Firey, Walter. *Man, Mind and Land: A Theory of Resource Use*. Glencoe, Ill.: The Free Press of Glencoe, 1960. Page 256.

2. Sears, Paul B. *The Ecology of Man*. Condon Lectures. Eugene, Ore.: University of Oregon Press, 1957. Page 40.

3. Hansen, Harry, ed. *The World Almanac, 1960*. New York: New York *World-Telegram* and *The Sun*, 1960. Page 307.

4. Spengler, Joseph J. "Population Threatens Prosperity," *Harvard Business Review*, Vol. 23, No. 1, 1956, pp. 85–94.

5. Gregg, Alan. "A Medical Aspect of the Population Problem," *Science*, Vol. 121, No. 3150, 1955, pp. 681–82.

6. Marsh, George P. *The Earth as Modified by Human Action.* (A last revision of *Man and Nature.*) New York: Charles Scribner's Sons, 1884. Page 629.

7. Powell, Major J. W. *Report on the Lands of the Arid Region of the United States.* Washington, D.C.: U. S. Government Printing Office, 1879.

8. Van Hise, Charles R. *The Conservation of Natural Resources in the United States.* New York: The Macmillan Company, 1910. Page 413.

9. Wooten, H. H. *Major Uses of Land in the United States.* United States Department of Agriculture, Technical Bulletin No. 1082, October 1953, page 11.

10. *Statement of Policy on Conservation of Natural Resources and Wildlife.* New York: American Petroleum Institute, 1961. Page 11.

Overpopulation and
Genetic Selection

FREDERICK H. OSBORN

All over the world, population pressures are being recognized as a threat to man's well-being. In India and Pakistan, where population pressures are already acute, the five-year development plans of the governments include large programs for reducing the rate of births. In the industrial countries of Europe the governments seem unconcerned; the people themselves continue to reduce the size of their families. In the United States the baby boom continues, but in a recent study (by Campbell, Tomasson, and Whelpton)[1] young married women, aged 20–24, indicated they expect significantly fewer births altogether than their counterparts five years earlier. There are many signs that the public is beginning to feel the pressure of too many people even in the United States. The question we are now considering is whether these pressures of population will, in the long run, affect trends in genetic inheritance.

GENETIC SELECTION UNDER PRESENT CONDITIONS

The most recent studies in the countries that have high birth rates and are suffering from heavy pressures of population show few appreciable differences in size of family as between different kinds of people. There seems to be no birth selection, but at the same time selection by differences in deaths is diminishing as the general death rate falls. Data in this field are limited by inadequacies of the census and the weakness of special studies that include only small samples of the population. But there is such a strong general agreement in the findings of all of the studies that as a group they can be given considerable weight.

The largest and most carefully developed study on differential fertility in China was made by Notestein and Chi-Ming Chiao on data collected in connection with the land utilization survey in 1929, 1930, and 1931.[2] In the areas which were studied the farms were rated according to their size in five groups, from the first group, which included all the smallest farms in each locality, to the fifth group, which included all of the largest farms in each locality. For the married women over forty-five years of age, those on the largest farms had the most children, as shown on the following table:

TABLE 1

THE FERTILITY OF MARRIED WOMEN BY CROP AREA OF FARMS
North and South China, 1929–31

		No. Women	Avg. Children Born
Group 1.	Small farms	1514	5.03
Group 2.	Medium farms	1697	5.06
Group 3.	Medium large farms	1845	5.28
Group 4.	Large farms	2284	5.35
Group 5.	Very large farms	2946	5.51

This study provides no information on the relation of mortality to size of farm. The people on the large farms would have an even greater advantage in survival if along with their larger families, their death rates were lower than the death rates on the small farms. That this may indeed have been the case is indicated by a small study by Griffing in 1926.[3] Questioning illiterate rural women in hospitals, he found that 164 women whose husbands had had five or more years of education had an average of 2.16 deceased children; 61 whose husbands had had one to four years of education had an average of 3.33 deceased children; and 220 with illiterate husbands had averaged 2.33 deceased children. At the same time average family size was greater among those with husbands having five or more years of education than among those with illiterate husbands, giving the more literate a somewhat greater likelihood of survival.

A number of studies have been made of the material in the 1931 census of India. The following table[4] is fairly typical of the results:

TABLE 2

RATIO OF CHILDREN 0–6 YEARS OLD PER 1000 WOMEN CLASSIFIED BY PERCENT LITERATE, BY CASTE. 1931

Percent Literate	No. of Children	
	Women 14–43	Married Women 14–43
15 plus	782	1030
8–14	800	1012
4–7	808	980
2–3	831	1007
0–1	869	1029

Most of the census studies show a higher fertility associated with the lower socioeconomic groups, with the lower occupations, and the less literate when all women 14–43 are included. But when only married women are included the differences are much reduced. They provide no information on differences in deaths and so tell us nothing about differential survival. It is possible that if deaths were included the more literate would be slightly favored for survival. In a number of other studies made in India, there is a consistent trend toward lower death rates among the more literate and upper castes.[5,6,7,8]

In both India and China at the time of these studies people of all classes were having large families, averaging five or six children per couple, and if there were differences in survival rates between different people with different degrees of literacy or education they were certainly small. There was little or no practice of contraception. Birth rates and death rates and their distribution were probably quite similar to those in previous periods of man's history, except for times of famine and epidemics when death exacted a terrible toll.

A new era was ushered in when death rates among European peoples fell as a result of improved nutrition, advances in medicine, and improvements in public health. The reduction in deaths was followed eventually by a fall in births, but since death rates went down first, European populations increased enormously in numbers. Births were reduced by the use of contraceptives, and in most countries contraception started among the upper classes and only moved down gradually. There was thus a long period when the more educated classes were having far fewer children than the less educated. A disproportionate number of children were being born and brought up in homes at the lowest educational level. There was concern that this would handicap educational improvement from one generation to another, and even entirely offset the influence of improvements in formal schooling which were being made at great expense. More recently, as birth control has spread to all levels of society, the differentials between different occupational groups in the United States have greatly diminished. Whelpton and Freedman, who have made the most recent studies on the subject, believe differentials associated with income, education, and place of residence show signs of disappearing.[9]

The quality of the home does not depend on social class, occupation, or income, but on the personal qualities of the parents. For this reason, as well as because differential fertility is now so reduced, the proportion of children being born in each of the different types of home environments in the United States today depends very little on class differences in birth rates, and a great deal on differences in size of family as between different kinds of couples within the same class or occupational group. Few studies have been made on this subject. We know very little about what kind of people are having more or less than their proportion of children. Having no evidence except that on class differentials, we can only assume that in the advanced countries with low death rates and low birth rates, the influences which determine size of family act equally on parents who provide "good" homes as on those who provide "poor" homes. We must make the same assumption for the less developed countries, where death rates and birth rates are still high, and where as we have seen there is evidence that all classes are surviving in about the same proportions.

If we think of the United States and other industrialized countries as areas of low population pressure, and of the underdeveloped countries as areas of high population pressures, there seems to be no evidence that population pressures of themselves directly affect genetic trends. In both kinds of countries the social forces which influence the distribution of births appear to exert their effect about equally on the competent and the incompetent, the educated and the uneducated. Neither past nor present experience gives us any guide to the future. We are in a period of rapid change, in which the fall in the death rate is spreading to major segments of the world's population, and birth control may be following some distance behind. Increasingly the human race is going to feel the pressures of a population growing too fast for the institutions that support it. We can only guess at the genetic consequences. But our guess can be based on an analysis of certain major trends in American life which directly affect the number of children born, and may affect what kind of children are born. The most important of these trends are the increased use of voluntary birth control together with constantly improving methods of control.

THE DIRECTION OF POPULATION TRENDS

Already today, some form of birth control is being practiced by over 90 percent of fecund American women who have been married fifteen years or more.[10] Present methods of contraception are in many ways unsatisfactory. Recently a pill has been approved for prescription by doctors which, taken orally for twenty days each month, has shown almost complete effectiveness as a contraceptive. In the laboratory stage are other physiological methods of control, from improved and cheaper pills to be taken less frequently, and by either men or women, to methods of immunization or vaccination. These new methods are not directly related, as are most present methods of contraception, to the actual act of sex. When such methods are used, the decision to have a child will be made at times of minimum emotional involvement. The result will probably be a substantial decline in the number of unwanted children. The social benefits will be considerable.

Illegitimate children are, for the most part, unwanted. Recently there has been a great increase in illegitimate births in this country. In 1938 the annual rate of illegitimate births was 7 per 1000 unmarried women age 15–44.[11] By 1957 it had risen to 20.9 per 1000 women, or something over 80,000 illegitimate births each year.[12] The rise was almost, but not quite, as great among white women as among nonwhites. If this rate continues we will have over a million illegitimate children aged 15 or under growing up in the United States. The chances are small that illegitimate children will have a satisfactory home environment. They are a burden to society and contribute far more than their share of problem children and juvenile delinquents.

There are many births of unwanted children among married couples today. Freedman, Whelpton, and Campbell interviewed over 2700 white married women between eighteen and thirty-nine years old, selected in such a way as to provide a sample of this group of the national population in March 1955. Among these couples, in a wide range of ages, 16 percent of the most recent pregnancies

57

were reported as not wanted by the wife, the husband, or both.[13] The authors feel that the answers to such questions probably provide low estimates of the number of couples who did not want their last pregnancy. The probability that the most recent pregnancy was unwanted increased rapidly with the number of pregnancies—from 6 percent for first pregnancies to 25 percent for fourth pregnancies and about 50 percent for the sixth pregnancy.[14]

Many, perhaps most, of these unwanted children of married couples get the same affectionate care as their planned brothers and sisters, but the family resources in time, health, and money available for the children may be strained by their presence. Some proportion of the unwanted children suffer to a greater or lesser degree from parental rejection. On the average the "unwanted" child, whether born in or out of wedlock, grows up in a less favorable environment than his "wanted" sibling. The situation of the unwanted child is increasingly recognized, and it probably won't be long before there is a demand that something be done about it. The public already has doubts about the way welfare payments appear at times to subsidize the birth of illegitimates, and is seeking means of helping illegitimate children without encouraging the birth of more of them. Success in reducing the birth of illegitimate children would probably be followed by attempts to reduce the birth rates of the shiftless and incompetent. There is already talk of the cost of carrying successive generations of incompetent families on the relief rolls. The public is increasingly being forced to recognize that, whatever the reasons, children, when they grow up, tend to be like their parents.

If the public really decides to put pressures on people

to keep them from having illegitimate and unwanted children, many means can be found. They will be increasingly effective as birth control methods improve. The pressures may be psychological, for people are much influenced by the atmosphere around them. There is a "fashion" in number of children as well as in clothes. The pressures may be institutional, such as the way relief payments are handled, or the extent to which the father is held responsible for the cost of his illegitimate child. They may be in the direction of public education which would give encouragement to social and welfare workers to advise the use of contraception. Many social workers today would lose their jobs if they were caught giving contraceptive advice. As the number of unwanted children went down, the proportion of wanted children would go up even if there were no actual increase in their number. But the fact of trying to reduce births among the shiftless might well lend urgency to the effort to increase births among the competent. Already we make special provision for the children of parents who are teachers in universities, or in government, or working overseas. This kind of help could be increased. Present tax laws allow an exemption of $600 for each child. If the exemption was based on a fixed proportion of income instead of on a fixed sum, the exemption would be of more benefit to couples who are ambitious for their children's higher education. By such changes and many others, by trial and error, and the study of the results of different changes, means could probably be found to tip the balance of births in favor of parents who will give their children a home environment favorable to their full development.

If the public demands changes of this sort, it will be

for environmental reasons. They will want the next generation of children to be born into the better home environments. At the present time the public would undoubtedly repudiate any proposals based on the desire for genetic improvement. They don't like to admit that genetic differences may account for part of the difference in the way people get along.

The interested geneticist, if he is wise, will not introduce the genetic argument. He knows that some part of the differences between people in any large group are due to the differences in their genetic makeup. He believes that even a small change in the proportion of genes favorable to intelligence and other socially valuable qualities would have results which would be cumulative from one generation to another. And he will be watching other trends which, in conjunction with selection, might have valuable genetic results.

Of particular interest to the geneticist are the trends toward increasing social and job mobility, toward the elimination of fixed hereditary classes, and toward giving everyone a chance at the best education he is capable of absorbing. These are all trends toward sorting people out according to their personal qualities, and putting each into the kind of life for which he is most fitted, whether as artists, businessmen, ministers, mechanics, lawyers, or manual laborers. Such a sorting out, coupled with the larger circle of acquaintance within which one may marry, favors an increase in the mating of like with like. Many studies have shown that, given the opportunity, men and women tend to marry people who are like themselves in physical appearance, coloring, intelligence, tastes, interests, and social background. Of course there are many exceptions, and people notice the exceptions. But all the statistical studies indicate that like tends to marry like, so far as the circle of acquaintance permits.

When our country was mostly agricultural, men married the girls they met on neighboring farms or in nearby villages. Their social background was likely to be the same, but the circle was small, and this limited the chance of their meeting girls whose personal qualities of mind or interests were like their own. Today there is a great deal of moving about, not only from place to place, but also from one social group to another. People far more than in the past are likely to find their own level of work or education and be brought in contact with people whose personal qualities are like their own. Under such conditions there is bound to be an increase in assortative mating. To the geneticist this is a matter of great interest; the genetic consequences may be far reaching.

Assortative mating, by changing the distribution of genes, makes for a greater number of people with particular and special qualities. It increases genetic diversification in the process of adapting to the diverse elements of our society. It should increase the proportion of people with a high order of specialized talent. If no selection is going on, it would also increase the proportion of the incompetent at every level of occupation; the proportion or frequency of each type of gene would remain the same, but the distribution would be different. We would have a more interesting but hardly a "better" society. It is quite likely that the genetic trend at the present time is along these lines, since we know there is a lot of assortative mating but there appears to be very little selection. If society should introduce an element of selection in births, the situation would be rapidly turned to advantage. Under assortative mating, particular groups of genes become concentrated in particular individuals. The decisions made by individual couples as to size of family become proportionately more significant. If certain genetic types of people have fewer children than the average, the proportion of such people diminishes from one generation to another. They would be selected against, and the frequency of their type of gene would diminish. On the other hand, if certain other types of people had more children than the average, their type would increase from one generation to another, and the frequency of their type of gene would increase.

Thus the natural trend toward more assortative mating in a mobile and complex society would make for genetic improvement if it were accompanied by a favorable selection of births. It would raise the level of specialized talents and at the same time raise the general level of each group in qualities common to achievement in any occupation. It would diminish, not increase class differences by raising the level of all classes.

It seems to the present writer that as the public increasingly feels the heavy pressure of a too rapidly increasing population it will react first with attempts to reduce births among the socially inadequate, and ultimately will want to find means for achieving discriminating selection of births throughout the population. So far as the public is concerned, it will be done for the sake of having children born into "good" environments. If such a change in public attitudes actually comes about the hardships inflicted by overpopulation will be offset by a major gain for the human race.

So far we have been dealing with genetic factors which

relate to intelligence and traits of personality. It is excellence in these qualities which enables man to master his environment. But at the present time geneticists are far more concerned with problems of genetic defect and susceptibility to disease than with the relation of genetic factors to intelligence and personality. They know more about genetic defects, and the problem seems more immediate.

THE GENETICS OF DEFECT

Individual differences range from differences in intelligence and emotional balance to physical differences ranging from vigorous good health to disabling defects. The extreme range of defects is the easiest to study; they are easiest to measure, and if they run in family lines they are most easily located. Further, they are of particular interest to a large professional group, the whole medical profession. For these reasons the individual differences most studied from a genetic point of view have been departures from the normal in the form of defective development, extreme susceptibility to disease, and mental defects arising from constitutional causes. Large-scale interest in this field developed among doctors after the Second World War, and greatly hastened the pace of investigation.

As a result of these studies we have come to realize that genes that cause defects are not limited to those families afflicted, but that many such genes are spread widely through the population. We have learned that the genetic consequences of artificial radiation, of lifesaving influences in medicine, and of new migration and marriage patterns are reflected in an accumulation of deleterious

63

genes over and above the subtle equilibrium previously established by natural forces. Methods are being devised to detect the individuals who are carriers of genes that cause defects as well as to treat some of the defects at an early age. Increasing medical knowledge and increasing public interest have led to the establishment of heredity counseling centers, and to a new recognition of the importance of heredity in human affairs.

It is generally accepted that genes that make for defect originate in so-called "mutations" which occasionally take place in one or another of the many thousands of genes that are present in pairs in every human cell. Usually the mutated gene is recessive, that is, it does not have its harmful effect unless the other gene in the pair has the same characteristics. The chances of two such genes meeting as a pair depend on the number of such genes distributed throughout the intermarrying population. Thus, if one person in a hundred carries a particular deleterious gene, the chances of his mating with a person with a similar gene are one in ten thousand. This may seem like a small chance, but in a large population such as that of the United States it may mean a great number of defective persons.

With every increase in the proportion of people who are carriers of a particular defective gene, there is an even greater increase in the likelihood of a mating in which two such genes will be paired in the same fertilized cell. When this happens there will be a defect. If the defect is lethal, the two deleterious genes will be taken out of circulation. If the defect is minor, but of a sort to make marriage or reproduction less likely, the genes are to that extent less likely to survive. Thus at some point nature establishes a balance in which, for every new deleterious gene brought into circulation, a similar gene is lost from circulation. The human race carries a considerable load of defect. Geneticists believe that most people carry at least a few deleterious genes—some geneticists put the average as high as eight—and at least two percent of the babies born into this world will carry all their lives some major or minor genetic defect. We get along just the same, but if the load became much heavier it might seriously threaten our future.

Most scientists are afraid that the proportion of carriers of deleterious genes may be increasing now quite rapidly —though the results in the form of a great increase in defect will not be apparent for several generations. Exposure to X rays and to fallout from atomic explosions is thought to be increasing the mutation rate, while at the other end, where failure to reproduce takes genes out of circulation, medical science is carrying an increasing number of people with some kind of defect through a period of successful childbearing. Diabetics for instance formerly died early, and the genes for diabetes were lost with them. After a cure was found in insulin, they survived and led useful lives, but were not generally able to have children. Now the safe delivery of the children of diabetic mothers is commonplace in our hospitals. The deleterious genes remain in circulation, and the proportion of diabetics is undoubtedly increasing from generation to generation. Of course we can get along with a lot more diabetics, and with good medical care they can live happily and bear diabetic children of their own. But there is a limit beyond which this process cannot be carried, and if we consider not diabetes alone, but all the other ills to which the human race is genetically heir, that limit is not far away. The fear of the scientists is that the accumulation of deleterious genes may creep up on us unaware and after a few generations increase the proportion of defectives to a point beyond the resources of the rest of the population.

Evidently the doctors and the public health authorities have a new and heavy responsibility. It cannot be carried out without an increase in public understanding. The current evidence from established heredity clinics indicates that couples will run a considerable chance of defective children rather than remain childless. Heredity clinics have been a great help to many anxious couples, but from a eugenics point of view it is hard as yet to assess their value. Perhaps a better education of the public in genetic matters will have the necessary effect. But we cannot rule out the possibility that any serious reduction in deleterious genes will not be possible by voluntary means alone. It would probably take a terrible increase in the proportion of people born with crippling genetic defects before the public would accept compulsory limitation of childbearing by carriers. Population pressures alone would not be enough to bring about such a change in public attitudes.

IN CONCLUSION

There is no present evidence to indicate that population pressures have an influence on those trends in births and deaths which would effect our genetic inheritance. But it seems reasonable to suppose that one of the public's reactions to population pressures will be to take a good look at who is having the children who will make up the next generation. If they do, there is almost certain to be a demand for a better selection of parents within every group of our people. By trial and error, experiment and careful study, means will be found for attaining a better discrimination in births. Improved methods of birth control, by pill or immunization, should then make for a fairly effective selection of births based on the voluntary decision of the parents. Present trends favoring assortative mating will make any form of selection more effective. Public health authorities will some day accept responsibility for genetic defect as they now accept responsibility for controlling contagious disease.

Population pressures may bring about genetic reform by intensifying the problems of civilization and forcing us to seek new solutions.

REFERENCES

1. Campbell, Arthur A., Tomasson, Richard F. and Whelpton, Pascal K. *The Reliability of Birth Expectations of U. S. Wives.* Paper No. 70 presented at September 1961 meeting of International Union for Scientific Study of Population, New York City, page 7.

2. Buck, J. Lossing, ed. *Land Utilization in China.* New York: Council on Economic and Cultural Affairs, 1937. Chapter V, "Population," by Frank W. Notestein and Chiao Chi-ming, page 385.

3. Griffing, John B. "Education and Size of Family in China," *Journal of Heredity,* Vol. XVII, No. 9, September 1926, page 332.

4. Davis, Kingsley. *The Population of India and Pakistan.* Princeton, N. J.: Princeton University Press, 1951. Page 76.

5. Datta, Subodh. "Differential Fertility in West Bengal in 1956," *Artha Vijnana* (Journal of Gokhale Institute, Poona, India), March 1961, pp. 67–83.

6. Chandrasekharan, C. *Mysore Study*. United Nations Population Division, The Government of India, 1961. Chapter 12.

7. Davis, op. cit., Table 26, page 78.

8. Gosh, D. and Veruna, Rama. *Study in Differential Fertility*. Proceedings of the Second All India Population and the First Family Hygiene Conference, Bombay 1938. Bombay: Indian Statistical Institute, 1939. Page 80.

9. Freedman, R., Whelpton, Pascal K. and Campbell, A. *Family Planning, Sterility and Population Growth*. New York: McGraw-Hill Book Co., 1959. Page 293.

10. Freedman, Whelpton, and Campbell, ibid., page 68.

11. *Illegitimate Births: United States, 1938–57*. National Office of Vital Statistics, U. S. Dept. of Health, Education and Welfare, Special Reports, Selected Studies, Vol. 47, No. 8, Sept. 30, 1960, page 227.

12. Ibid.

13. Freedman, Whelpton, and Campbell, op. cit., page 75.

14. Ibid., page 73.

FRANK FRASER DARLING is a graduate of Midland Agricultural College and received his PH.D. at the University of Edinburgh, when he later became senior lecturer in ecology and conservation. He also holds doctorate degrees in science and law and is a Fellow of the Royal Society of Edinburgh. He is now vice-president and Director of Research of the Conservation Foundation. From 1944 to 1950 he directed the West Highland Survey in Scotland, and in 1952 published his major work, *West Highland Survey: A Study in Human Ecology*. In addition to many articles on animal ecology he is the author of more than a dozen books on wildlife, ecology, and agriculture. Among them are: *Pelican in the Wilderness, Odyssey of a Naturalist, Herd of Red Deer*, and *Wildlife in an African Territory*.

The Population Explosion
and the Natural Environment

FRANK FRASER DARLING

Small and primitive populations of mankind achieving their own subsistence do not enjoy long periods of leisure, and such as they have is markedly of the social sort, in and about the home and the village place, gentle in bodily effort or vigorous in dance and play. A later stage, arriving at civilization, may result in much leisure for the privileged and much less for the general run of folk. There comes a cultural stage when folk show a remarkable degree of staying in their own place. As hunting declines in importance and agriculture imposes its own authority, the immediate environment may be markedly changed but beyond the fields lie the forest and waste, as the old words have it, where the folktales tell of many dangers known and unknown. Tribal cultures also tacitly accept the notion of wide buffer areas between peoples where nature holds her own.

The Neolithic revolution made permanent aggregation possible, and the Iron Age made a considerable impact on the natural environment because charcoal was needed for smelting. As populations gradually increased and iron production became specialized, the impact grew more severe. Scottish forests were felled in the seventeenth and eighteenth centuries to smelt English iron. England, that former country of oak forests, had lost her timber. That kind of impact did not end till the Bessemer coke furnace stopped charcoal burning completely in countries where coal existed. So some forest returned to Sussex and the Kentish Weald.

Despite the rise in population in a country like Britain and the establishment of the industrial North, there was, to an extent still to be documented historically, a lessening of the impact of man on the countryside of parts of England in the nineteenth century. Railways canalized travel, and the country districts away from them were in a backwater. Depopulation of rural areas began, roads declined in quality, and coaching inns went empty.

New England can tell a similar story of rural activity declining with the colonization of the much better lands farther west. The country is now back in timber and its value as recreation ground for the densely populated eastern seaboard is accepted. Impacts lift and shift about the world. Pastoral scourges come and go, as the transhumant flocks of the Mesta in Spain, sheep and cattle in the United States' western mountain country, and in much of the pastoral Middle East of Asia, where they have impact on the natural environment which becomes almost permanent. The United States, after a century or less of wrong usage, has made valiant attempts to reverse the effects of fire and tooth, but from the Sahara to China the semiarid pastoral belt shows one of the most spectacular changes brought about by man on his environment.

Erupting hordes of human beings and folk-wanderings have been a phenomenon of world history and pre-history. The famous Wenner-Gren Conference at Princeton in 1955 resulted in 1000 pages of a remarkable book, *The Role of Man in Changing the Face of the Planet*. But we are now up against something new in the eruption of population and the behavior of people. I want to confine myself to a situation in the most highly materially civilized countries which is growing rapidly more complex and needs greater socioecological analysis than it is getting. None of us knows very well how to investigate effectively the new phenomenon of spread of human wear and tear over more or less natural countryside of all kinds, shores, mountains, forests, and even deserts, which are so rarely absolute deserts. The quality of surface tension referable to mass production and such services as public education, which brings about urbanization and depopulation of rural areas, is one aspect of the trend of change, but the new hard use of the natural environment in weekend and holiday exodus is like a sudden storm flood in its impact.

One could analyze it in this way: Rousseau waking up an opinion despite the nonsense he wrote and talked; the Romantic poets, Blake, Byron, Coleridge, and Wordsworth; men like Thoreau, and then a spate of Hudsons, Jeffries', Muirs, Teddy Roosevelts, Ernest Thompson Setons, and lots more of us who have written about natural history and wild country. Not only has there been a population explosion but an eruption of opinion toward what is called "enjoyment" of the out-of-doors. Opinion alone would not have got people around, but the slightly lagging concomitant of mass production and now automation is increasing leisure. To the bare increase of population must be added the increase of leisure hours as an additional factor of impact, impelled by the new, basically healthy outlook and propelled by the internal-combustion engine. The internal-combustion engine has become the wild card in this demographic game of poker and assumption of a poker face of unconcern is certainly not going to help us win the game of saving scenery, wilderness, or what we call beautiful country.

Railways canalized travel and quietened the back country. Now, railways are largely on the way out and new highways and rejuvenated old roads have penetrated in such fashion that countries and continents are carved up and rendered into a pattern of geometrical islands. A new motor expressway is as much of a biological barrier as a mile of water. Rural areas and natural environments (whatever that term may mean) are reeling under a shock of usage which it is doubtful they can adapt to and survive. I do not wish to dwell particularly on the fate of mammals and birds: they can move (while there is anywhere left to move to), and they have powers of resilience and adaptability. Scenery has none as far as I know, and vegetational communities cannot take themselves somewhere else. Vegetation has certain powers of comeback and as it is the clothing of much scenery, a certain measure of manipulation is possible, but vegetation with its attendant communities of small, unconsidered invertebrate animals is clothing which can be slashed and rubbed into holes both consciously and unconsciously, and by not knowing what is happening. It is scarcely conceivable that any American would shoot a loon, but the loon has gone from that part of Yellowstone Lake where dashing about in noisy outboard-motor boats is allowed. Lots of people crystallized that kind of scenery in the sight and sound of the loon; the internal-combustion engine as the handmaiden of leisure could reduce the loon to a folk memory, to a decorative symbol on the brochures of the resort proprietors. There are several lakes in Alaska from which the loon has gone already.

The National Parks system of the United States is respected the world over and has been the spearhead of thought in this direction for nearly a century. I take the Parks now as an example of pressures on wild lands which are in what might be thought to be the favored position of being dedicated to remaining in their primitive state. The establishment of twenty-nine National Parks covering 13½ million acres of some of the most spectacular scenery on the continent cannot be credited to public demand, but to the farsightedness and public spirit of a few men. Public appreciation has come later with the possibility of visiting remote areas which the internal-combustion engine in the motorcar has made possible. There has been constant and bad-tempered pressure on the Parks from commercial interests for water, timber, grazing, and the less desirable forms of recreational concession. Resistance to this danger has been remarkably successful so far, though there is no lessening of the danger, and the recent severe threat to the Dinosaur National Monument showed that public opinion which had lagged in the formative years could now be depended upon to defend the National Park system.

But the internal-combustion engine has called round to collect its price of support: a foolish metaphor it might be said, but I use it because each of the occupants of nearly all the motorcars visiting a National Park is a humble, decent citizen expressing some of the marked national idealism by being there at all. His only shortcomings in such surroundings are that he has physical weight and proceeds by friction, that he has needs of food intake and excretion which in our civilization are attended by complicated land-and-labor-using services, he has to lie down at night, and his motorcar takes up an appreciable fraction of an acre of ground space. It also has an alimentary system of sorts demanding contraptions and services which do not add to the wild beauty of the scenery. There were nearly 63 million visits to National Parks in 1959, and 80 million are expected by 1966.

Putting aside the truths of Parkinson's Law, it is not generally realized how insidiously large communities can build up in places where normally a town would not grow. The very roads, which when well made and well kept maintain the movement of traffic, demand men and machines in their service. The machines need service and fuel, the men need food and shelter, their children need schools and schoolteachers. And every activity of service calls for its own particular services, so that the apex of a visit of enjoyment of a National Park rests on a wide pyramidal base of people, buildings, and what not. A physically narrow beauty spot like Zion Canyon cannot adjust itself to meet the demands put upon it. The geyser area of the Yellowstone is already a special kind of slum city.

Sometimes this kind of pyramidal build-up cannot be accepted by the climatic nature of the country, whatever may be dictated by physical shape. Death Valley in California is extremely arid and is the home of a special subspecies of the bighorn sheep. Water is so scarce, and the visitors and their services are now demanding so much of it in this National Park, that the desert bighorn flock is being pinched in its modest and minimal demands. Do we accept the extinction of the sheep and put up a pictorial notice board explaining that this is where they were before visitors became so numerous as to use all the water?

The National Park Service has been headed by some wise men who have done an imaginative job of canalizing the traffic, and building in such a fashion that the scenery is not violated. Therefore, a large amount of back country remains in good order for anyone prepared to use his legs. But Mission 66 is a planning effort aimed to cope with increased patronage of the Parks. My own impression is that the good taste of the past is being departed from in some of the new construction, and some of the idealism which has characterized the National Park Service is being forced into retreat. I am not so much criticizing a harassed public body as trying to impress the very great problem arising from the increasing desire and ability of increasing populations of people to "enjoy" a finite amount of space.

The feeling for wilderness is growing, and though few of us can have that very necessary forty days within it, many more are reaching what are called wilderness areas. The internal-combustion engine gets the devotee to the periphery, and he thereafter takes the trail, either with pack-horses or carrying his own load. Trails are the natural best ways of getting through country, often being paths originally made by wild animals. Moderate use maintains such trails, but a seasonal heavy activity of the passage of hundreds of horses makes the trails into severe dust hazards for the nasal sinuses and into erosion gullies when the rains come.

Many mountainous areas in the United States are now being subjected by the internal-combustion engine to a penetration which would not have been imagined a few years ago. There may be neither roads nor original tracks, but blithe and adventurous spirits have devised a low-geared motor scooter with which it is possible to climb around in a seated position, with the legs and feet busily used as fenders and fulcral points in twisting and turning round the obstacles. These machines, replacing the timber-cruiser's slow horse picking its way, are also creating erosion hazards.

I have used the National Parks System of the United States as an example of the pressure of people on wild country because it is a big country thought to contain a lot of room and not too many people. But the cult of mobility is farthest advanced, with one motorcar for three people, cheap gasoline, and an undoubted prestige element being cultivated in both mobility and the motorcar.

Other countries also have their problems: 7 million people took a seaside holiday in Britain in 1939; now it is 30 million. The coastline of England shows the strain on the habitat, and even when the Pembrokeshire National Park was established, essentially a measure for saving coastline, it was violated within a few years to build an oil refinery at Milford Haven. Political trends abroad and development at home demanded it.

National Parks in Britain are restricted special planning areas. Sanctuary for animals and plants and the scientific conservation of distinctive habitats is the duty of a Privy Council research body, the Nature Conservancy. The problems of beating industry, exploitation, and development in the race to acquire sites varying from a few acres to several thousand are bad enough in themselves, but the care of the habitats calls for more than scientific management through ecological knowledge; there remains the problem of people. Entry to most of the National Nature Reserves is by permit, an irritating business in itself, but entry has to be regulated in numbers also because the treading of human feet can do a lot of damage in certain types of forest and fen. Do not the aspens die around the picnicking places at the side of United States roadways in National Forests? In the forest of Fontainebleau in France it is necessary to fence round at several yards' radius some of the magnificent old oak trees. The pressure of many feet upholding the bodies of ardent admirers of nature and the out-of-doors would kill the great trees. No exploitation here, just admiration, and the habitat cries out for a barbed wire fence! (The durability of that special habitat, the urban savannah typified by Hyde Park and Hampstead Heath, needs study, but perhaps we can thank the damp climate which gives it such long spells of rest.)

More people with growing leisure for recreation are already pressing heavily on what are called natural and wild areas. Conservation has here one of its biggest tasks for the future, to manage the habitats on the one hand, but on the other to take up its share of the social and administrative responsibility.

PART II

Population Pressures on Economic and Political Trends

EUGENE R. BLACK has been president of the International Bank for Reconstruction and Development since 1949. A graduate of the University of Georgia, Mr. Black has had an impressive career in the field of banking in Atlanta and New York City. He resigned in 1949 from the senior vice-presidency of Chase National Bank. Mr. Black served for two years, 1947 to 1949, as the United States Executive Director of the International Bank for Reconstruction and Development.

Population Increase
and Economic Development

EUGENE R. BLACK

There are movements in the less developed countries which vitiate all efforts to raise world living standards. One of the most massive of these obstacles is the tremendous rise in the populations of already crowded countries.

For every four persons on earth in 1950, there are today five. For every five today, in forty years there will probably be ten. In the past half minute alone, about ninety babies will have been born into the world; only sixty persons will have died, leaving a net increase of thirty, or one every second. This rate of growth last year added the equivalent of the population of Italy to the world's millions, and the rate seems to be accelerating. In 1962 it will probably push the population of the world past the three billion mark, and it will double that figure before the end of the century.

Three hundred years ago there were probably no more than 500 million people alive in the world, and the total was increasing only slowly. This stability was maintained by an uneasy balance between high birth rates and death rates. Many babies were born, but many also died. Living conditions were such that many of the remaining children failed to survive beyond the age of thirty.

In Europe, the picture began to change in the late eighteenth century. Populations began to grow, sometimes very fast. Elsewhere, the balance of new lives against deaths has been upset largely in our own lifetime. The pattern has been a steep fall in death rates, with birth rates little changed. But the circumstances have been somewhat different from the earlier European experience. The population revolution has often been achieved very cheaply. In Ceylon, to take the best-known example, the expenditure of two dollars a head on a public health campaign with the prime purpose of eradicating malaria reduced the death rate by three quarters over a single decade. Similar stories can already be told of public health programs undertaken in other countries, and there will undoubtedly be more in the future.

Of course we welcome this trend, whatever the problems it may set for us. We all want to reduce the suffering and waste involved in premature death or disabling disease, and we can expect death rates to go on falling in the developing countries. Medical science continues to discover increasingly effective ways of promoting public health, and since governments can usually act on behalf of the community in putting these new techniques to work, we may expect them to be applied as soon as the money can be found to pay the accompanying bill. People will live longer in the future.

But if only twenty people—or even fewer—in every thousand are henceforth to die each year, then a birth rate of forty per thousand, which formerly just kept the population steady, will bring an explosive growth in numbers. And there is little reason to suppose that birth rates will soon decline to match the fall in death rates. It is much simpler to attack disease than it is to alter the reproductive pattern of a society. Medicine has yet to make available a cheap and easy method of regulating births. And not everyone wants fewer children.

What view are we to take of all this?

I am not convinced that population growth will eventually outrun the development of the world's resources. It is true that at present rates of consumption we will use up the known reserves of several important fuels and minerals within a few decades. Heavy demands will certainly be made on our agricultural resources, and there may be acute difficulty in organizing the movement of food and other necessities about the world on the scale required to meet the needs of a population twice its present size. But I am inclined to think that those prophets who forecast the exhaustion of the earth's resources, underestimate the ingenuity of man and the potentialities of science. And I am not too disturbed about the long-run problems of feeding the extra persons we expect, although I find myself a little out of sympathy with some of our professional agricultural optimists—it seems to me Utopian to expect that every country will be cultivated as efficiently as Denmark, and that thereby the world could easily feed twice its present population.

But all this does not mean that we ought to welcome population growth on the scale that we see it today.

Some people argue that a big population implies a good

market for the businessman's product: he can use mass production techniques and charge low prices. They insist, too, that with a growing population, the businessman constantly finds demand exceeding his estimates. Optimism and production run high; new products win ready acceptance, while obsolete industries die painlessly; the incentive to invest is strong; and social mobility and change are encouraged. The burden of social costs is spread widely. By contrast, they suggest, a declining or even stationary population brings pessimism and economic stagnation; there is insufficient reward for private enterprise, and the state is thereby forced to intervene increasingly in fields better left to the private citizen.

This body of theory may conceivably be true in the circumstances of a rich country with resources to spare. But it is wildly irrelevant to the problems of most developing countries today.

It is, of course, a fact that some of the poorer countries do not have domestic markets big enough to support mass-production industries. But it is clearly ridiculous to suggest that inadequate population is holding back the development of, say, India, which packs more than twice the population of the United States into less than half the space. Where most people go barefoot for lack of shoes, industry is not failing to grow because its products are not wanted. Where the agricultural laborer can find work to occupy him for only half the year, no further pressure is needed to make him wish for a different occupation. Where two thirds of every dollar of income must be spent on food, where manufacturing industry is almost nonexistent, one need not worry that excessive saving will lead to underemployment of resources. The lash of further poverty is not required to drive these people to action. The developing countries need many things—not only capital, but the skills and health to make good use of it. By no means do all of them need population growth.

But need it or not, they have it. They should ask themselves if they can afford it. In Asia, in the Middle East, in Latin America, in Africa, the population of most countries is growing at the rate of 2 percent annually—and sometimes 3½ percent or more. In some parts of Latin America and Africa there is fortunately room for the extra people. In the long run, although not now, there should also be adequate resources available to feed, clothe, and house them. But in many parts of Asia and the Middle East, resources are few, and there is not nearly enough room. Agricultural land which once sufficed to support a stationary and much smaller population has already been divided and subdivided beyond the limits of effective cultivation. Cities are crowded to bursting, and are still getting bigger.

Population growth on this scale would be a serious challenge to a country with adequate living standards. Where incomes are very low, and economic development is a desperate need, such growth can be a crippling handicap.

The speed at which a country develops depends largely upon its ability to direct its growing resources to investment rather than to consumption, to uses which will raise tomorrow's output rather than satisfy today's demands. A poor society finds it difficult to save at all, and will be doing well if it can set aside 10 percent of its income. At this rate, if its population is growing, it will be investing barely enough to stay where it is. Yet the likelihood must be that it will invest not more than 10 percent, but less: a growing population with a high proportion of dependent children will find it increasingly difficult to spare any of its income.

Unless foreign aid can be increased, a country in this position is faced with a stark alternative. It must reduce its savings, or lower its living standards—although both are already inadequate.

The industrialized countries have shown their willingness to help. Common humanity and self-interest alike impel them to do so. All the evidence points to a greater flow of aid in the coming years. But I find myself increasingly doubtful whether domestic savings and foreign aid together will be sufficient to allow real progress, if present rates of population growth continue for long.

Figures are hard to come by in this field. But it may be possible to indicate some orders of magnitude.

Some calculations have been made about the cost of providing houses in India during the next generation if the population continues to grow at its present rate of about 2 percent a year. If you disregard the cost of rural housing, on the somewhat optimistic assumption that it can be carried out entirely with local materials and labor, then you still have to pay for the homes of nearly 200 million extra people who, it is expected, will be living in India's cities twenty-five years hence. Making full allowance for the fact that many of the extra persons will be children needing not new houses, but simply more space in existing households, a sober estimate of the cost suggests that in the thirty years between 1956 and 1986 a total investment in housing on the order of 118 billion rupees, or roughly \$25 billion, will be needed. If you find a figure like that difficult to grasp, I may say that it is well over four times the total lent by the World Bank in all countries since it started business fifteen years ago. Put another way, it is more than thirty times the initial resources of the International Development Association—and those resources are supposed to cover IDA's first five years of operations.

My cost estimate takes no account of the need to improve existing housing in such cities as Calcutta. It leaves out the cost of roads, sewage systems, water supplies, and other services. Yet the problems of urban growth form only a small part of the challenge presented when economic development is attempted in the context of a vast expansion in population.

In the social field, many more new hospitals and clinics will be needed, simply to maintain present standards—standards which by common consent are sadly inadequate. Far more must be spent on education. Here look again at India, not because its problems are unusual, but because they are well documented. In 1956 about 31 million Indian children were getting an education—less than 40 percent of those of school age. It is mathematically certain that if the population grows as expected, a three- or fourfold increase in educational investment will be needed if all children are to be receiving an education by 1976. When you come to productive investment, the story is similar. Enormous investments will be needed. But population growth does not only tend to reduce the flow of investment funds. It also means that the capital invested in industry must be spread increasingly thin over the labor force: each pair of hands is backed by fewer dollars of capital. Productivity suffers, and the gap in living standards between the developing and the industrialized countries widens, instead of narrows.

I must be blunt. Population growth threatens to nullify all our efforts to raise living standards in many of the poorer countries. We are coming to a situation in which the optimist will be the man who thinks that present living standards can be maintained. The pessimist will not look even for that. Unless population growth can be restrained, we may have to abandon for this generation our hopes of economic progress in the crowded lands of Asia and the Middle East. This is not a field in which international agencies can do much. But there is scope for governments to act: it is time that they gave earnest attention to this threat to their aspirations.

Population growth does not alter the rules for successful economic development. On the contrary, it reinforces their strength by increasing the penalties for breaking them. In relation to the need, capital is short, and must be stretched as far as it can possibly go. In the developing countries, therefore, the first question to be asked of any economic policy must be, "Is this the road to maximum economic growth?" and if the answer is "No" we must look very closely at any doctrines that are put forward to excuse this sacrifice of economic advancement.

For the providers of economic aid, this situation implies a duty not only to see that the money is properly and efficiently applied, but also to guard against the temptation to use development assistance to achieve their own commercial or short-term political objectives, rather than to serve the priority needs of the recipient countries. For the developing countries themselves, it implies that they must realize that they least of all can afford to accept low returns on their investments. They cannot afford to waste scarce resources by putting prestige ahead of real need, by ignoring hard economic calculations, by refusing to accept productive capital while they debate for years the respective roles of public and private enterprise.

At best, and even if real sacrifices are made by the industrialized nations to increase the flow of aid, there is grave danger that, in the face of existing rates of population growth, the resources available for economic development will fall short of the needs of the developing countries. We bear a heavy responsibility toward succeeding generations to make the best use of all our resources.

EARLE L. RAUBER, vice-president of the Federal Reserve Bank, Atlanta, since 1952, received his education at the University of Chicago (PH.B. 1924, M.A. 1925, and PH.D. 1930). From 1930 to 1943 Mr. Rauber taught economics at the Alabama Polytechnic Institute. In 1943 he joined the Federal Reserve Bank, first as a senior economist and then director of research.

Industrial Growth
in the Twentieth Century

EARLE L. RAUBER

The current competition between the United States and the Soviet Union for the support of nations just emerging from colonial status as well as of other underdeveloped areas is serving to focus world attention upon a problem of vast importance. The problem lies in the explosive growth of population precisely in those areas least able to support it.

In an age of scientific marvels and of industrial and engineering miracles, it is baffling to realize that of the earth's nearly three billion inhabitants, nearly two billion, mostly in Asia, Africa, and Latin America, are subsisting on less than enough nutrition to maintain health and vigor. Into these underdeveloped countries, where birth rates have always been high, and where they still remain so, modern medicine has entered with its latest knowledge of epidemiology and its panoply of disinfectants, insecticides, vaccines, and antibiotics and has thereby succeeded in suddenly and drastically reducing death rates. The net result has been an increase in population beyond what could be supported on any reasonably adequate level of living by existing resources and within the framework of existing social, political, and economic institutions. There has thus come about an increase in the mass of world poverty that is an offense to the conscience of mankind and an affront to its intelligence.

Whether or not the problem of raising the living standards of these impoverished billions will be solved by the nations of the free world, or by those of the communist bloc, or even by both together, is a question that only history can answer. In the meantime, however, one thing seems certain. Unless the gap between birth rates and death rates is closed in areas of growing population pressure, all efforts for their relief and progress may prove futile. The rising demands of multiplying billions of people could conceivably overwhelm the capacity to satisfy them, whether those of the free world, the communist world, or of both.

This problem is not remote as far as the United States is concerned. It is one that touches all of us, for it is the billions of dollars that this country channels into foreign economic aid that constitutes the chief contribution of the free world to the alleviation of world poverty.

If, despite our aid, this poverty continues to grow worse because of an uncontrolled growth of population, then the drain on American resources may be expected to increase. Such a contingency should prompt us to look to our own productive capacity and to the demands that our own population is making upon it. The United States is today undoubtedly the wealthiest nation in the world and enjoys a standard of living higher than any in all history.

Although there is presently no serious threat to this position, it would, nevertheless, be wise to be on the alert to possible signs of difficulty in the future.

During most of its life the United States has been fortunate in the possession of vast land areas and other natural resources and of a small but vigorous population. This combination of circumstances, together with the fact that nearly every area of economic endeavor was being invaded by the spreading industrial revolution, meant that labor was very productive in this new country and that wages were therefore high compared with those in Europe and elsewhere.

High wages and abundant opportunities to escape from the wage relationship into businesses of one's own had two important effects on the development of the country: they attracted to our shores a large stream of immigration at a time when additional hands were an economic asset, and they stimulated the substitution of machinery and other forms of capital for the relatively scarce labor. The result was a rapidly growing population on the one hand, but a still more rapid industrialization of the country on the other.

The rate of population increase was the greatest, of course, in the early decades when population was small in absolute terms. In 1800, for example, the population was 5.3 million and in 1810 it was 7.2 million—an increase of 1.9 million, or 36 percent, in a ten-year period. The decade-to-decade percentage increases remained in the 30s up until the 1860–70 decade when the increase fell to 23 percent. It rose to 30 percent in the following decade but thereafter began to decline until it reached a low of 7 percent in the decade 1930–40.

Surprisingly, however, what at the time had seemed like a permanent decline in the population's rate of growth was then reversed. Between 1940 and 1950 population increased by 14 percent and between 1950 and 1960 by 19 percent. This dramatic upturn of the population curve now raises some fundamental questions concerning the relation of a population's size to its economic well-being.

Without having recourse to overly refined statistical techniques, we may nevertheless arrive at some tentative answers to these questions. The facts of economic life are, of course, bewilderingly complex in detail, but their broad relationships are fairly simple and easy to grasp.

For our present purpose, the two most essential magnitudes to consider are, first, the physical output of goods and services that the economy produces and, second, the number of people who share that output directly or indirectly. Since most economic magnitudes are commonly stated in monetary terms, however, the effect of changing prices must first be removed from the monetary aggregates before we can see what is happening in the world of real things.

If we consider the years from 1929 through 1960, we see that they fall into a few well-defined periods: a four-year depression period, 1929–33; an eight-year New Deal period, 1933–41; a five-year war period, 1941–46; and a fourteen-year postwar period, 1946–60.

During the four-year depression period, the nation's annual output of goods and services valued at current prices, the so-called Gross National Product, fell from $104 billion in 1929 to $56 billion in 1933—a decline over the four-year period of some $48 billion in the annual rate, or at an average rate of $12 billion a year. During the eight-year

New Deal period this magnitude rose at an average rate of $9 billion a year; during the five-year war period, it rose at an average rate of $17 billion a year, and during the fourteen-year postwar period at an average rate of $21 billion a year. Summarizing this development, we can say that in monetary terms the nation's output of goods and services was over five times as great in 1960 as it was in 1929. Deflating this figure with the consumers price index (1947–49 = 100) in order to eliminate the effects of price changes, the real output in 1960 was a little less than three times that of 1929. This is the outside dimension of the nation's prosperity.

The rate at which real or physical output has been changing can be expressed by saying that during the New Deal period (1933–41) it rose by $12 billion a year, during the war period by $11 billion a year, and during the postwar period by $10.3 billion a year—a declining rate of increase. To put it another way, the average annual increase in physical output in the postwar period has been 18 percent less than what it had been in the New Deal period.

Turning now to population, we find that during the depression period the population increased on the average by a million a year and during the New Deal period by only 900,000 a year. During the war period, however, it increased by 1.6 million a year and during the postwar period by a phenomenal 2.7 million a year—a rate not far below 2 percent a year.

The effect of these population increases on the position of the individual can be discovered by dividing the figures representing physical output by those for population, thus converting them to a *per capita* basis. When we do this we discover that during the New Deal period the average annual increase in *per capita* physical output amounted to $85, in the war period it amounted to $59, and in the postwar period to $30. On a *per capita* basis, therefore, we find that the average annual increase in physical output in the current postwar period is 65 percent less than it was in the 1933–41 or New Deal period.

Here again the picture is one of a declining increase in *per capita* productivity. Indeed, if population and real Gross National Product continue to behave in the next five years as they have so far in the postwar period, the average annual increase in *per capita* physical output will fall to $22. Increases in *per capita* productivity would therefore seem to be declining in the direction of a point at which there would be no increase at all. The gains from further expansion and technological improvement in industry would all be absorbed in the support of additional people and the level of living would cease to rise. We would then, indeed, have entered the realm of the Red Queen in Lewis Carroll's *Through the Looking-Glass* where, as the Queen remarked, you have to run as fast as you can to stay in the same place, and if you want to get somewhere else you have to run twice as fast.

The danger point could be reached uncomfortably soon if the rate of population growth was to suffer a further increase and if *per capita* investment in capital failed to grow or were to lag. If, however, population growth were reduced to the rate prevailing before the Second World War, and if *per capita* investment in capital were stepped up from current levels, the danger point might be postponed indefinitely.

The obvious conclusion to be drawn from all this is that

even a very high degree of industrialization such as we have achieved in the United States is in itself no guarantee of perpetually rising levels of living for individual citizens, even though it may tend to swell all economic magnitudes to larger and larger proportions. The industrialization of the United States, as we have seen, occurred in a combination of almost uniquely favorable conditions and we thus became a nation of unprecedented national wealth and individual material well-being.

The sudden turnabout in the birth rate since the late 1930s, however, has brought the United States for the first time in its history under the shadow of Thomas Malthus. Over a hundred and fifty years ago Malthus foresaw that in a race between productivity and reproductivity, reproductivity, if unchecked, would win out in the end. In the United States, it is our good fortune that population growth is catching up with the growth in productivity while we are still at a very high level of national and individual well-being.

It is the misfortune of the world's underdeveloped countries, however, that reproductivity is there winning out in the very short run. Population is there outpacing the ability to support it at a time when productive capacity is still at a very low level because of the late and rather tenuous development of modern industry and all its supporting institutions. Abysmal poverty, therefore, with all its customary unlovely stigmata is the inevitable lot of the vast majority of the people.

If, on the one hand, we in the United States and other highly industrialized countries can keep our rates of natural increase within bounds and so avoid using up our economic surplus merely in the support of additional numbers, we may be able not only to safeguard our own high level of living but also to contribute substantially to the industrialization of the countries that so desperately need it.

On the other hand, if those countries fail to reduce their birth rates to something commensurate with their death rates, but, on the contrary, allow increases in productivity to be consumed in a further increase in numbers, then whatever aid we might give them toward their industrialization could easily end in an increase in the mass of human poverty and misery rather than in the elevation of human living conditions.

In the case of the underdeveloped countries at one end of the economic scale, industrialization alone is not sufficient to create better living conditions, nor, in the case of the United States, at the other end of the economic scale, can it assure the permanence of present levels of living. In the one case as in the other, the control of population growth is essential to the future welfare of all of us.

In countries where it has been given a congenial home, modern industry has conferred many and great benefits upon mankind. It can continue to do so in the future, but only if its largess is not atomized by being spread over increasing multitudes of recipients.

LORD BOYD ORR is an internationally known food expert. He is a Knight of the British Empire and Fellow of the Royal Society and received his M.A., M.D., and D.SC. at the University of Glasgow. He was made Rector of Glasgow University in 1945 and Chancellor in 1946. Lord Boyd Orr has served in an advisory capacity for many government committees and was Director General of the United Nations' Food and Agricultural Organization from 1945 to 1948. He received the Nobel Peace Prize in 1949. He is the author of *Food and the People* and *The White Man's Dilemma* and has contributed several papers on physiological subjects to scientific journals.

Mankind's Supply of Food

LORD BOYD ORR

The explosion of population began in Western Europe about the middle of the seventeenth century. From 1 A.D., the beginning of the Christian era, until 1650, the average rate of increase was only about 150,000 a year. But then began the accelerating rate of growth which now threatens our civilization.

By the nineteenth century the new rate was well under way. In England, for example, between 1800 and 1900 the population increased from 9 to 35 million, not counting the millions who emigrated. During that century the world average rate of growth rose to 4½ millions a year, the main increase being in Europe and in the new continents to which Europeans had emigrated.

Between 1800 and the year 1924 when the United States imposed quotas on immigrants, nearly 60 million Europeans left for the new continents. This relieved the pressure of population on the land in Europe, and food from the fertile virgin lands of the new continents supplemented the increased yield of home-produced foods and saved the people of Europe from starvation.

Since the beginning of the present century the accelerating rate of growth, due mainly to the control of disease, which reduced the death rate with no corresponding reduction in the birth rate, has spread to nearly all counties. By 1946 the rate had risen to 22 million a year. In the early 1950s it was up to 30 million. Today it is 50 million and it is estimated that within twenty years it will be 75 million. Unless there is a rapid fall in the birth rate there seems nothing to stop it reaching 100 million.

There are now no new sparsely populated continents to take the overspill of population which saved Europe in the eighteenth and nineteenth centuries. And soil erosion, which since the beginning of our predatory civilization has destroyed about half of the once fertile land of the earth, continues, in spite of the soil conservation policies of some countries.

There is little wonder that this rising tide of population and falling reservoir of sources of food production is causing anxiety among people who have any regard for the kind of world their grandchildren will inherit.

The main worry of writers on the population problem is the food supply. Consider how much will be needed. If, in international politics, governments were as much interested in promoting the welfare of the people of the world as their prestige and material interests camouflaged as a conflict between communism and capitalism, their first joint concern would be to cooperate in abolishing hunger and malnutrition. In 1946 it was estimated that taking account of the anticipated increase in population world food production would need to be doubled in twenty years to provide an adequate diet for all the people in the world. The position is not much different today. Increase in food production has done little more than keep pace with increase in population. Two thirds of the people in the world are still ill nourished.

The population is increasing at a rate which will double it in less than forty years. If the present accelerating rate continues, in eighty years when many infants of today will still be alive, the present population of 3000 million will be well over 12,000 million. Therefore, to provide an adequate diet would require more than eight times the present world food supply.

Could that amount of food be produced? On that there are different views. My own is that with modern engineering and agricultural science it is physically possible to increase the food supply more than eight times. But that could be done only under two conditions. The first is that all governments would be willing to cooperate on a world scale for its increase and equitable distribution. The second is that all governments would contribute in proportion to their resources, estimated by the amount of money devoted to military budgets, to an international fund to provide for the vast amount of industrial goods needed mainly by the undeveloped countries for the rapid increase of their food production. It would take at least 12,000 million dollars a year to provide sufficient food for all people within about ten years. That is about 10 percent of what the world is spending on military budgets.

Is there any hope that such a miraculous change could take place in international relations? Two events in the past suggest that it is possible. Before the last World War, in the League of Nations created by the idealism of a great American President to replace recurring wars by cooperation for the promotion of the welfare of the people, twenty-two nations, including America and Soviet Russia, had delegates at a conference considering a world food policy based on human needs. The war brought that movement to an end. Then through the idealism of another American President the Hot Springs Conference was called during the last war to get international cooperation in a food policy to abolish hunger from the world and raise the standard of living of the people of the undeveloped countries. This policy was approved at an international conference in 1946, but when government delegates met six months later to draw up the plan of action the Great Powers were not prepared to give any funds or authority to any international organization for any such purpose.

Is it too much to hope that the new President of the United States might have the vision to call another Hot Springs Conference and convince the world that this time the United States would be willing to cooperate in carrying through the decisions of the conference?

If the United States fails to do this, then the hope of the world may be with Soviet Russia, the only other nation with the power and prestige to induce nations to cooperate in such a worldwide plan.

Leadership in the world today depends not on the government that has superiority in hydrogen bombs, which no one can use without committing suicide, but on the government that can induce all governments to take the first step from the agelong era of recurring wars with hunger and poverty for the majority of mankind to the new atomic age of peace, abundance, and world unity.

If no government is wise or astute enough to take the lead in this movement, then my hope is that as the standard of living and education rises in the undeveloped countries where the rate of increase in population is greatest, the fall in birth rate will occur as it did in Europe. Failing that, my hope is that governments will realize the danger of the present rate of population growth and cooperate in a world movement to use pills, which are or soon will be available, to reduce fertility of women or men or both.

If these hopes are merely wishful thinking with no substance to support them, then I am inclined to agree with Sir Charles Darwin that we are living in the twilight of a golden age and that even if we escape annihilation in another world war our civilization will collapse in chaos through the burden of population which the earth can no longer support.

My belief, however, is that these hopes are well founded and that the present explosion of population and the other dangers which modern science have created are merely the birth throes of a new age of stabilized population in a world of peace and plenty.

Environmental Planning
for an Increased Population

SOLLY ZUCKERMAN

There is only one kind of history one can glimpse before it is written. It is the little we always seem to extrapolate, however vaguely, from those few trends of man's social evolution which some inner conviction tells us have been defined for all time. Even so, our extrapolations have to be treated with caution; we all know how often the path of obvious prediction has been diverted by unexpected and hidden obstacles. But however cautious, one simply cannot avoid believing that all men, whoever they are, and wherever they live, will go on striving to better their material lot, that standards of literacy and education will continue to rise throughout the world, and that world population will be vastly greater at the end of this century than it is today. It is out of the question not to accept these propositions. They are the major facts of our time, and to deny them would be sheer irresponsibility on the part of informed people. We can hardly fail to accept that in our century it is mainly the pressure of the many, and not the actions of the few, which is determining the way the world is going.

Most of those who are contributing to this volume have in their lifetime seen the population of the world increase from an estimated 1600 million at the beginning of the century to about 3000 million today. Less than forty years hence, in the year 2000, the number is likely to be 6000 million. Nearly a four-times increase in a hundred years. The broad facts and implications of this rate of population growth have been spelt out in other chapters, and I have been asked to address my remarks to the topic of environmental planning. If this concept is to mean anything in the future, we have to begin by remembering that there has been all but none of it in the past. The history of our exploitation of natural resources—and in particular of land and water—is essentially a series of individual responses to immediate needs and desires and not the unfolding of some master plan indicating what was likely to prove best for all people in an undisclosed future. We have also seen our world transformed, not only by the increase in the numbers of its inhabitants, but also by the ever accelerating pace with which new science and new technology have transformed our material environment. A thousand different influences have interacted to bring about the pattern of life as we know it. Everywhere we see growing industrialization, higher material standards of living, ever sprawling, crowded cities, traffic congestion, widening disparities between the have countries and the have-not countries—all occurring under a system in which we improvise as well as we can in handling the problems yesterday unwittingly created for today.

"The essence of genius," someone has said, "is to align

oneself with the inevitable." Reasonable estimates suggest a doubling of the world's present population before this century ends. How do we adjust to such a fantastic absolute increase in our numbers? What shape do we wish the inevitable to take? To plan means to control, or at least to qualify, the main determinants of our future. Let us suppose that the search for some effective physiological means for slowing down the growth of population proves successful and that world population in the year 2000 is not 6000 million but, say, 5000 million. We would still be left with the problem of planning our physical environment to deal with an increase of 2000 million people over the next forty years. In relation to what has gone before, this still will be an immeasurably difficult thing to achieve. How is it to be done? How will it be done? For clearly it will have to be done.

Obviously the problem will be tackled differently in different countries, in accordance with the nature of their political institutions. Given they are farsighted, countries living under authoritarian regimes will by definition find planning easier than those whose democratic institutions are designed to preserve the principle of laissez-faire. The problem of transforming our physical environment will also be tackled with greater urgency in some than in other countries, for the pressure of new population is likely to fall heaviest on the poorest, who will be least able to deal with the problems of catering in an orderly way for a burgeoning population. The United Kingdom, which present estimates suggest has a population of about 53 million, may come off lightly, crowded though it already is. Forward projections suggest that its population will still not number quite 65 million by the year 2000. Projections such as these, however, have a habit of proving wrong.

But in all countries, and whatever their manner of government, providing an environment for the many cannot but curtail the liberty of the few. This is simply a consequence of greater crowding. Those of us who live, and prefer to live, in the institutions of democracy will have to get ready to see our own liberty to do as we please, in the pursuit of our own interests, becoming even more subordinated to the needs of society at large than it has been over the years. Unless we accept this, our industries, our roads, our cities will never develop in such a way that they can cope with twice, or nearly twice, the number for which they are now designed. This is inevitable. The siting of new factories, of new roads, of new towns, has already become transformed into a series of major political issues in all the countries of the West. Environmental planning to deal with a rapid doubling of the world's population will inescapably be associated with, and almost become a concomitant of, political and economic change. Even if there is a nuclear holocaust in the next decade or two, this still seems inevitable.

Man's wants are unlikely to change unless his physical and physiological makeup changes. This cannot happen in any time scale within which it is reasonable to try to cast one's thoughts. He will need food, shelter, clothing, heat and power, space in which to live, leisure and opportunity for travel. Modern technology will obviously change the way some of these needs are satisfied, but it is hardly likely that the needs themselves will be changed in any essential feature. As standards of living rise, both in already industrialized and particularly in the unindustrialized parts of the world, more raw material will be required to support an individual, more food, more metals, more timber, more chemicals, and more utilizable energy and knowledge. These requirements will be inevitably associated with changes in our environment. Because of possible developments in nuclear technology, it begins to look as though the demand for energy will be the easiest need to satisfy. As our need for raw materials fails to be satisfied from sources which we now regard as economic, the availability of cheap power will make it possible to exploit those which, by present standards, are not. Eventually the world may well have to sustain itself, as has been pointed out by Dr. Harrison Brown, on "materials obtained from the rocks of the earth's crust, from the gases of the air and from the waters of the seas." Provided the science and technology are there, this is not impossible.

However much we may turn to unconventional quarters for the satisfaction of human needs, the most important problem will remain the provision of food and of renewable resources such as timber and other forms of cellulose. Land, which is already in short supply in many parts of the world, is likely to grow even scarcer as population grows. The pull of higher standards of living seems inevitably to draw people to the centers of cities, and it seems improbable, therefore, that those forces which today urge people to depopulate areas such as the Highlands of Scotland will cease to operate. The proper planning of land-use today is thus the most urgent problem in the planning of the environment of tomorrow. The conventions of land tenure which apply in many parts of the world, and even the architectural tastes to which, in one shape or another, we are now bound, will have to be modulated by the inexorable pressures which the necessary use of our land resources implies. It would be far cheaper to resurrect the deserts in the effort to help house the world's population than to stimulate large-scale emigration to other planets—a fantasy that has already cropped up in the world of space fiction.

So far as environmental planning is concerned now, the most urgent implication of population pressure today is that we try not to make man's future more difficult by an overemphatic perpetuation of habits and conventions which are not vital to our well-being. The likelihood that world population will double within fifty years is a more significant fact than most, if not all, of our present preoccupations. If the democracies are to avoid the rigid blueprints of totalitarian states, the closer the accidental circumstances which determine action today can therefore conform to what people ultimately come to regard as design, so much the better for the environment of the future. In this sense the problem of population pressure becomes simply a problem of politics and leadership.

HENRY STEELE COMMAGER, educator and authority on American constitutional and intellectual history, received his education at the University of Chicago (PH.B. 1923, A.M. 1924, and PH.D. 1928). He began his teaching career as an instructor in history at New York University. In 1938 he joined the history department of Columbia University as a professor and remained there until 1956, when he left to become chairman of the Department of American Studies at Amherst College. Dr. Commager's works include *The Heritage of America, Living Ideas in America, The American Mind,* and *Freedom, Loyalty, Dissent.* Also, he has edited a number of books on American History.

Overpopulation and the New Nations

HENRY STEELE COMMAGER

The nationalism of the eighteenth century was a humane and civilized affair. It was a product of history rather than of calculation, it was dynastic and territorial rather than linguistic or religious, and it was cosmopolitan rather than chauvinistic. It was an era when aristocrats, philosophers, artists, and scientists could move freely from country to country, even in time of war: when Goethe could wear French decorations and Sir Humphrey Davy cross the channel to Paris to receive the gold medal of the French academy in time of war, and Napoleon's mother keep her money in British consulates; when George III could retain the American Benjamin West as his court painter, and Franklin bespeak immunity for Captain Cook, and Benjamin Thompson (Count Rumford) become a British Colonel, Prime Minister of Bavaria, a citizen of France, and leave his fortune to found the Rumford chair at Harvard College.

There were frequent wars, but they were dynastic and, for the most part, they were fought by professionals and mercenaries. There was a good deal of shifting about of territory, but rarely massive destruction of city or country-side, or heavy loss of life. Tiny armies fought over vast territories in the American forests or on the plains of India, but losses—except through disease and desertion—were small.

Modern nationalism came with the French Revolution, and with it modern warfare as well: mass armies, conscription, heavy losses, something like total war. The era of modern nationalism—from 1789 to the present—has been one of almost continuous warfare—warfare between the great powers of the Old World, warfare in Africa and Asia. For modern nationalism sought not only colonies, but resources and markets as well, and sought these by conquest. The nineteenth century has been peculiarly the century of imperialistic expansion and of titanic conflicts for control of great continents and the trade routes to and from them—imperialistic wars that grew and grew until with the Second World War they became veritably global in character and scope.

The emergence of modern nationalism and of imperialistic expansion coincided with—and was indeed a consequence of—the first great increase in population in modern history. The population of Europe was roughly 150 million in the year 1700; by 1789 it had increased to roughly 170 million, and by 1815, even with a quarter century of war, to perhaps 200 million. But a hundred years later it had more than doubled—in 1914 it reached 460 million—and this with a migration of between 40 and 50 million over the previous century. The explanation is obvious enough: improved medical and health facilities, and an increase in resources, natural and manufactured, through the application of science and technology to agriculture and industry.

Most of this immense increase went into the rapidly growing cities of the Old World; some of it headed for the wide open spaces of the Americas. Corn from Iowa and wheat from the Argentine helped feed the new urban proletariat, while the incessant demands of underdeveloped countries gladly took the products of their industries. But America was soon producing for herself, and there was a limit to what Asia and Africa and South America could absorb. So competition for control of these old-new continents grew sharper and sharper; competition for resources and, ultimately, for food, grew sharper and sharper. The relationship between expanding population, imperialism, and warfare is perhaps the most elementary fact in modern history.

Now it is Asia, Africa, and South America that are experiencing the population explosion, and it is in these continents that we are witnessing the upsurge of chauvinistic and imperialistic nationalism. These ancient peoples are throwing off colonialism and imperialism—and embarking upon their own imperialism. They are revolting against the West, but with the tools and instruments of the West —the political tool of nationalism, the economic tools of science and technology. China—victim of the greatest population explosion—is pressing hard on all her neighbors and may precipitate warfare not only along her own borders, but throughout Asia. Pakistan and India are acting not unlike Italy and Austria in the nineteenth century; the Arab lands—not yet suffering from heavy overpopulation—are pressing hard on Israel and on their European colonials. In the Congo, in Cuba, in Indonesia—wherever on the globe the ratio between population and resources gets too desperately out of hand, chauvinistic nationalism takes over and threatens disorder and war.

But there is this to be said about the wars of the nineteenth and the wars of the twentieth century. In the nineteenth century, small countries like Denmark or Portugal or Greece could not really launch a major war, and even European wars, devastating as they were, did not threaten the safety of the globe. But now a small country like Korea or Egypt or Laos can involve great powers in wars; now small countries with advanced technologies—a Denmark, an Israel, a Hungary—can build and use atomic weapons. Modern warfare is more contagious than nineteenth century warfare, and it is more dangerous.

If the newly emerging nations of Asia and Africa adopt the chauvinistic nationalism of the nations of nineteenth-century Europe, the outlook for civilization is grim.

Is there any chance of mitigating the ravages of this new nationalism?

Something can be done—and is being done—through the good offices of the United Nations. Something is being done through the beneficent work of such organizations as the World Health and the World Food organizations. Something is being done more directly by the foreign-aid programs of the United States and Russia.

But the fundamental problem is to eliminate or relieve the intolerable pressures that are driving the new nations to violence. It is essential to increase production, but increase in production has not so far—except perhaps in Japan—brought relief, for with increased production goes an increase in population. And with increased production, too, goes—ordinarily—a more advanced science and technology that embraced improved public health programs designed to cut down the death rate. The prospect that confronts us, therefore, is one where population increase is outstripping the increase in production.

Only a resolute and comprehensive program of limiting population can provide that breathing space so essential to countries like China, India, Pakistan, Ceylon, the Congo, Brazil, Indonesia, and many others, if they are to bring their resources up to a level with their population. Only if we can somehow persuade them to provide this breathing space can we hope to avoid those convulsive gestures that will inevitably lead to a new round of nationalistic wars and that may destroy the great globe itself.

GRENVILLE CLARK is an authority on disarmament and various aspects of world law. He began his career as a lawyer with a New York City law firm in 1906 after receiving his Bachelor of Laws from Harvard. He has received Doctor of Laws degrees from Harvard, Princeton and Dartmouth. Mr. Clark has written *A Plan for Peace* and is co-author, with Louis B. Sohn, of *World Peace through World Law*.

Population Pressures and Peace

GRENVILLE CLARK

The main purpose of this article is to stress the close interrelationship between the problem of the "population explosion" and the problem of world order.

I shall submit the proposition that a solution of the problem of keeping populations within tolerable bounds is largely, and perhaps decisively, dependent upon finding a way to terminate the arms race and to bring about a better-ordered world, while the question of organizing peace will, in turn, be much influenced by success or failure in solving the population problem. I shall suggest, therefore, that those especially concerned with the mitigation of population pressures and those concerned with the effort for genuine peace should more clearly recognize the close interdependence of these problems and should cooperate to the fullest extent.

At the outset, I make clear that in speaking of "peace" I use this elusive word in an intermediate sense as meaning something more than the mere absence of actual armed conflict, but something less than an ideal and tranquil world in which all international disputes can be resolved by agreement and without the aid of a well-organized system of enforceable world law.

On the one hand, I cannot regard as a condition of "peace" the state of affairs existing in late 1961 in which two great rival blocs confront each other armed to the teeth, while exchanging daily insults. On the other hand, the "peace" I speak of will not necessitate a highly developed "world government" but will require those minimum world institutions corresponding on a world scale to the basic legislative, executive, and judicial institutions shown by the experience of centuries to be essential for the maintenance of law and order in local communities and within nations.

What I call "peace," as above defined, can be realized, I conceive, only when this concept of enforceable world law in the limited field of war prevention is generally accepted. And, more specifically, I believe that this "peace" requires nothing less than a comprehensive plan, including the following elements:

1) *Universal and complete disarmament,* by which is meant the literal abolition under an adequate inspection system, of all national armed forces and armaments by every country in the world, without prejudice to the maintenance of agreed-upon police forces for internal order only, strictly limited in number and very lightly armed.

2) *An adequate world police force,* meaning the establishment, parallel with the disarmament process, of a strong and heavily armed force composed of volunteers and not of national contingents, with careful safeguards against possible abuse of power by this force.

3) *A world judicial, quasi-judicial, and conciliation system,* under which impartial world tribunals would be established in order to provide fully adequate means for the peaceful settlement of *all* international disputes, without violence or the threat of it.

4) *World law-making and executive agencies,* so constituted as to be fair to all nations and also workable in practice, the powers of these agencies to be carefully restricted to those essential for the prevention of war.

5) *A world development authority,* adequately financed and staffed, to mitigate the vast and excessive economic disparities between the have and the have-not nations.

6) *An effective world revenue system* to provide reliable revenues for the maintenance of the world police force and other necessary world institutions, since without such a system the mere establishment of those institutions would be a futility.

I cannot emphasize too strongly that every one of these elements is essential. For it is no more sensible to expect world order without *all* these world institutions than it would be to expect a watch to keep time without every one of its interrelated parts.

By "population explosion," I mean the prospective doubling of the world's population over the next fifty years, from approximately 3 billion at the end of 1961 to about 6 billion in 2012. While well aware that various estimates indicate a doubling of the 1961 population in forty years (barring all-out nuclear war), I am inclined to believe that various influences will slow down the recent rate of increase so that a doubling to 6 billion is more likely to require fifty years. But whether the population increase to 6 billion occurs in forty or fifty years is not crucially important. In either event the problem is formidable; and beyond fifty years I do not seek to look, in view of the many unpredictable discoveries almost certain to be made in our fast-moving era.

When I speak of keeping populations within "tolerable" bounds, I mean such control of the population of any particular nation that its national product, fairly divided, can provide barely enough food, clothing, and shelter for all its people, together with minimum medical care and enough education to make most of its people at least barely literate. And here I emphasize that the population problem does not primarily relate to the mere global increase in the number of people, but rather to the distribution of that increase. Thus various large countries (including the United States, Canada, and Australia) could doubtless maintain at a good standard of living, populations even three times as large as those of 1961, while, on the other hand, even a doubling to 900 million of the population of India or to 1300 million of that of China would almost surely prevent any important betterment of the dire poverty of their people. In short, the real problem is not so much to prevent a large increase in the population of the world as a whole, but rather to concentrate on the prevention of even moderate increases in areas already poverty stricken and obviously unable to provide for even the minimum needs of larger numbers.

In terms of money (1961 dollars), I take this to imply that for a population to be within "tolerable" bounds its per capita income must be within the range of $200–$300 per annum, depending upon the climate, soil, and other living conditions of the particular area. I suppose this minimum to be the very least which can supply the bare essentials for a minimum standard of living. And, therefore, when reminded that, through its new Five Year Plan, India hopes by 1966 to raise the per capita income of her then estimated 492 million people from $69.30 to $80.85, I would reply that this simply demonstrates that India's population with relation to her resources would still be far beyond any "tolerable" limit and that this situation demands radical change.

The truth is that the below $100 per capita incomes of China, India, Pakistan, and a number of other countries, having in 1961 an aggregate population of at least 1400 million persons, are a disgrace and reproach to the rest of the world. As contrasted with the economic condition of the nations of western Europe with their per capita incomes of $900 to $1400 (not to speak of the $2300 per capita income of the United States), the situation corresponds on a world scale to the disparities between the haves and the have-nots which preceded the French and Russian revolutions. In our modern TV age, the poverty-stricken masses will no longer remain ignorant of these glaring contrasts and will no longer be resigned to their situation as the common lot of mankind. Nothing is more certain, therefore, than that these conditions will be radically altered, the only question being whether this change will occur through peaceful means made possible by massive and long-term aid from the industrialized nations, or through violent upheavals which will shake the world.

It also follows that an imperative task of the industrialized West is to see to it that the average incomes of the masses in all the very poor areas of the world are at least doubled within no more than a generation, a task imposed by self-interest as well as by a decent regard for the welfare of their fellow human beings.

With these definitions and assumptions, my inquiry narrows and can be stated as follows: First, what effect will the establishment of the minimum institutions requisite for world order, or the failure to establish them, have upon the problem of keeping population growth within tolerable bounds over the next fifty years? Second, what effect will the assumed doubling of the world population within fifty years have upon the achievement of genuine peace through total disarmament and enforceable world law?

Concerning the first question, it seems plain that a continuance of the present vast expenditure of at least $120 billion per annum on the arms race and the Cold War would seriously, and perhaps fatally, handicap the effort to control the population explosion.

The principal influences which restrain population growth appear to be a fairly high standard of living, usually the result of industrialization, and a considerable degree of literacy; while, by contrast, very fast population growth tends to be associated with extremes of poverty and lack of education. Thus a recent writer on China who speaks of "new generations being born at an awesome rate in the face of terrible adversity," could have said with equal truth that this increase is *because of* that very adversity.

It seems to follow, therefore, that in order to bring under control the populations of China, India, and those other countries in Asia, Africa, and Latin America in which population growth presses most heavily on available resources, there will need to be a *highly organized, persistent, and costly* effort to promote industrialization and education. The conclusion is inescapable, I submit, that only a *massive and prolonged* effort of this sort will suffice to enable the people at large in those areas to acquire not only the motive but also the knowledge to induce them to practice family limitation.

It is also very clear, I believe, that the Western world is now merely trifling with this situation. The United States did, indeed, in August 1961 announce a program of prospective aid to Latin America amounting to $20 billion over a ten-year period, and this was hailed as a liberal and even epoch-making program. And yet, when we consider that the population of Latin America during that period will probably average at least 230 million, we see that even this program will provide less than $10 per capita per annum.

Again, we hear of a possible United States aid program for India and Pakistan of some $1.5 billion per annum. But when this is analyzed, having in mind their 1961 combined population of about 530 million, it appears that this would come to less than $3 per capita per annum, an amount which cannot possibly bring about any important improvement in the standard of living among those teeming masses.

Still more striking is the utter inadequacy of aid from the "have" countries to China with its 650 million people and a per capita income usually estimated at not over $75. In this case, because of the Cold War, the Western bloc provides no aid whatever, so that whatever assistance is received comes wholly from the Soviet Union and other countries of the Eastern alliance and almost certainly does not exceed $2000 million per annum, or say, $3 per capita.

What is plainly required is a coordinated program

whereby *all* the industrialized countries will contribute for the improvement of economic and social conditions in *all* the have-not countries, not $10 billion per annum, but not less than $50 billion per annum over a long period of years. Having in mind that any such program would only be feasible through a strong world organization, a plan of this sort, to be carried out through a World Development Authority under a revised United Nations Charter, was proposed by Professor Louis B. Sohn and this writer in our book *World Peace through World Law*.

The proposal there made is that this World Development Authority would be financed through a world revenue system whereby the United Nations could have an annual budget equal to 2 percent of the estimated gross world product in any year. Taking 1980 as an example, a gross world product of $2600 billion was assumed for that year, thus permitting a maximum United Nations budget of $52 billion, which after allowing, say, $11 billion for a strong United Nations Peace Force and other expenses would permit the allotment of $41 billion to the World Development Authority for aid to all the have-not areas of the world without discrimination. Subsequent study and reflection have, however, convinced us that the problem of the have and the have-not areas of the world, as affected by continued population growth in the poorest areas, requires a more drastic treatment. And, in consequence, we propose in the new edition of our book that the maximum budget of the United Nations in any year may be equal to 3 percent, instead of 2 percent, of the estimated gross world product in that year.

The result would be, again taking 1980 as an example with an assumed gross world product in that year of $2600 billion, that the maximum United Nations budget could be $78 billion, of which some $65 billion could be made available to the World Development Authority. As applied to the probable 2.5 billion people of the world then living in dire poverty, this would be little enough, at only about $26 per capita, to bring about any great improvement. The point which I wish to enforce is that upon no less terms than these can the population problem be successfully dealt with. We must radically "raise our sights" if continued misery and possible great catastrophes are to be prevented.

The other side of the coin is that success or failure in the organization of peace under effective world law may be largely determined by the outcome of the efforts to control the population explosion. The most important reason I take to be that, with population outrunning resources in large areas of the world, and with consequent unrest among hundreds of millions of impoverished people, the difficulty of organizing and maintaining peace might be sharply increased. Thus the already formidable task of agreement upon a comprehensive plan for peace might be made still more difficult, and almost certainly the task of maintaining peace, even after the achievement of total disarmament and the establishment of the necessary world institutions, would become harder.

Consider, for example, the case of China, which, even with her 1961 population of some 650 million, looms as a threat to world stability. Is it not possible that by 1980, when that population may well have reached 900 million, the pressure to obtain new territory for their support would be extremely strong? And in a highly competitive world, even after total disarmament, would not the existence of so vast and impoverished a population make for constant rivalry for its adherence and thus for continued international tension? At the very least, it seems clear that, if the effort to keep populations within tolerable bounds is making good progress, this success will be a favorable influence toward the organization of world peace under world law and for the maintenance of that peace without undue friction. On the other hand, if the efforts for population control are proving a failure, it seems probable that the unrest and apprehensions thus created would gravely handicap the effort for the organization and maintenance of peace.

In summary, I submit as the principal inference from this analysis that the effort to keep populations within tolerable bounds during the next half century will be very greatly, and perhaps decisively, affected for good or ill by the success or failure of the effort to achieve genuine peace. This is so, I believe, because if the effort for world order is successful, that success will greatly facilitate the effort to control the population explosion by releasing from the arms race immense material resources and human energy to promote industrialization and education in the have-not areas of the world, which would, in turn, operate greatly to reduce population growth.

A second inference is that failure in the effort to control population growth will substantially hinder the effort for a peaceful world, since continued large population increases in already impoverished areas would inevitably tend to instability and to intensified struggle for control of those areas and, hence, to still more tension which would handicap the struggle for peace.

A final and obvious inference is that the workers for

population control and the workers for peace, the world over, should more clearly recognize the close relation between their respective problems and should consciously and actively coordinate their efforts.

Let those concerned with the population problem concern themselves equally with the effort for total worldwide disarmament under enforceable world law, which is the only road to genuine peace. And, correspondingly, let the workers for an ordered world recognize the importance of the population problem as affecting the effort for peace and actively assist the concurrent effort for population control. By such a coordination of talent and resources, the prospects for a better-ordered world and for a better life for its people can, I suggest, be immensely improved.

The Menace of Overpopulation

ARNOLD J. TOYNBEE

In our time we have seen a drastic reduction of the death rate, especially of infant mortality. This has been brought about by the progress of preventive medicine in conjunction with progress in public health administration. The beneficent effects were felt earliest in countries that were relatively advanced economically and socially, but the reduction of the death rate has now become virtually worldwide. This has been one of the finest achievements of modern civilization, but it has created a serious new problem: How, in the new circumstances, is an explosive increase in the world's population to be prevented? The only way of preventing it is to reduce the birth rate more or less in proportion to the now achieved reduction in the death rate. But, unlike the death rate, the birth rate cannot be reduced by compulsory public measures, administrative and medical, of a relatively simple kind. It can be reduced only by the voluntary private action of millions of husbands and wives, taking individual decisions in a matter that touches one of the most intimate sides of life

135

and that raises delicate questions of custom and even of religion.

In spite of these difficulties, the birth rate has, in fact, already been reduced in countries in which the levels of prosperity and education are relatively high. Consequently, in these countries, the increase of population is being kept within limits within which it does not prevent an increase of welfare. These countries, however, contain only a small minority of the human race. In most of the world, the birth rate is still as high as ever. Consequently, in these countries the uncounteracted reduction of the death rate is producing an increase in the population which is offsetting, and threatening to do more than offset, the increase in productivity resulting from the introduction of modern technology. In these countries the increase in productivity and the increase in population are, alike, new developments. Both are due to the impact of modern civilization. But the modern gift of preventive medicine is canceling the beneficial effects of the modern gift of technology.

As a result of the failure to reduce the birth rate in the indigent countries, as contrasted with the success in the affluent countries, the gap between the respective standards of the indigent majority of the human race and the affluent minority is at present widening. This is politically dangerous. It threatens to divide mankind into two camps: a majority camp of increasingly resentful have-nots and a minority camp of increasingly uneasy haves. This accentuation of the extremes of wealth and poverty as between different sections of the human race is not only dangerous, it is also uncivilized and inhumane. It runs counter to the present movement, inside each of the more advanced countries, for reducing inequalities in wealth and opportunity. The contrary tendency on an international scale is disturbing. We cannot resign ourselves with equanimity to its continuance.

The problem is how to persuade husbands and wives in the indigent majority of the human race to adopt birth control voluntarily. This is bound to take time. It has taken time even in the more advanced countries. This is inevitable, because the change requires a break-away from age-old habits which, in some societies, have been consecrated by being given a religious sanction. All over the world until recent times, human beings have bred up to the limit, as an insurance against the huge toll taken by disease and war. Till recently, this toll was so high that breeding up to the limit was necessary in order to secure the survival of the human race. The reduction in the death rate, brought about by the effective introduction of public health measures, has produced a sudden revolutionary change in an age-old state of affairs. But ingrained habits, answering to that now obsolete state of affairs, cannot be changed so quickly or so easily, in spite of the fact that, in the new circumstances, these old habits have ceased to be salutary and have become deleterious. Even if we do eventually succeed in persuading the whole human race to change these ancient habits, this process of voluntary self-education is going to take time.

This raises the question: How much time do we have for carrying out this vast and formidable educational enterprise? Evidently there is going to be a race between the increase in the world's population and the increase in its food supply. Even if a substantial reduction in the birth rate is achieved eventually on a worldwide range, the time lag between the achievement of this and the already accomplished fact of a substantial reduction in the death rate is going to produce an increase in the world's population which will be staggering, even if we succeed in keeping it down to a minimum. The population experts estimate that, at a minimum, the world's population will have more than doubled before the close of the present century.

Fortunately the world's food production can be increased considerably by the application of modern science. Some people have been so impressed by the possibilities of this that they have persuaded themselves that the population problem can be ignored. "Let population soar," they say. "Science will be able to provide food for any conceivable increase in the number of human mouths to be fed." This cannot be true, for the human race, like every other species of living creature, will increase its numbers ad infinitum unless and until the increase is artificially checked. On the other hand, there must be a limit to the increase in the supply of food for human consumption, even if science is allowed to do its utmost. Therefore, sooner or later, when science has done all that it can do, the unlimited tendency of population to increase will necessarily be curbed. The only open question is regarding the way in which this inevitable limitation is going to be brought about.

In the past, the increase in human population, like the increase in the population of other species of living creatures, has been checked by the action of impersonal forces. Two such forces that have operated on all species alike have been pestilence and famine. Human population has also been kept down by a third scourge, war, which is impersonal, though man-made. The question is whether we should now allow human population to expand till it is checked again by one or all of these ancient scourges, or whether, before that disastrous point is reached again, we should check the growth of population ourselves by a planned limitation of the birth rate.

Surely there can be no question about the choice that we want to make. We do not want ever again to leave it to nature to regulate the size of the world's human population in her wasteful and heartless way. Nature's way is to let both the birth rate and the death rate run at a maximum. But, from man's standpoint, this way is inhuman and subhuman. It is an offense against the value of human life, which is a corollary of the dignity of being human. It would be intolerable for us to relapse into a regime in which the maximum number of human beings would again be brought into the world in order to provide a margin for allowing the maximum number of premature deaths—the majority of them in infancy. What we want is to bring into the world the optimum number of human beings, neither more nor less. And, in this context, the optimum number means the number that will give the best possible life—best in the spiritual as well as in the material sense—to each individual. From our human point of view, human beings are the most precious beings on this planet. They are persons who have human rights. They are not expendable.

This is one of our fundamental human articles of faith. It is therefore our moral duty, and our social responsibility, to make as sure as possible that it shall be put into practice. It would be irresponsible in the highest degree to let the growth of human population take its natural course and to trust blindly to the progress of science to provide food for an endlessly increasing number of human mouths.

People who put this blind trust in science seem to forget that science cannot actualize even its limited potentialities unless it is liberated from the political restrictions that are hampering its operation today. President Kennedy, in an address to the two Canadian houses of parliament, pointed out that Canada and the United States, between them, could produce enough food to feed the whole present population of the world at an adequate level of calories. This may be true, but the possibility cannot be actualized unless the food produced in North America is given away gratis to other parts of the world, or, alternatively, the people in these other regions are provided with effective purchasing power. Nor can the world's food supply be raised to its potential maximum so long as the earth's surface is partitioned among a hundred sovereign independent states, each with its own currency, own tariffs, and own import and export quotas. In order to raise the world's food supply to its potential maximum, the whole habitable and cultivable surface of the planet will have to be thrown together into a single unit for the purposes of food production and food distribution.

This is politically practicable. It was actually achieved for a few years at the end of the Second World War and just after it. During those years, an international authority, the United Nations Relief and Rehabilitation Agency, was allowed to take control over the whole of the world's food supply and to ration this to the whole of the world's population. UNRRA made itself responsible for ensuring that no one in the world should starve, and it discharged this tremendous responsibility with remarkable success.

As soon as the immediate wartime crisis was over, UNRRA was liquidated. This beneficent institution for the welfare of mankind as a whole was sacrificed on the altar of nationalism. But, before the end of the current century, a new UNRRA, armed with overriding powers in its own field, will surely have to be set up if the statisticians' present minimum estimates of coming population growth turn out to be right. This new, and this time permanent, UNRRA is perhaps likely to be the first genuine executive organ of world government that mankind will create for itself. This seems probable because hunger is a still stronger power than nationalism.

PART III

Population Pressures
in Specific Areas

WALTER C. LOWDERMILK is an internationally known expert on soil conservation and land management. He received his B.A., B.S., and M.A. at Oxford and his doctorate in 1929 from the University of California. He has served as a conservation and land development adviser to Israel, Morocco, Tunisia, and the British colonies in Africa, and on the President's Water Resources Policy Commission. Dr. Lowdermilk's books are: *Tracing Land Use Across Ancient Boundaries; Palestine, Land of Promise;* and *Eleventh Commandment.*

The Promise of Agriculture
in the Less Developed Lands

WALTER C. LOWDERMILK

INTRODUCTION

Civilization is running a race with famine and the outcome is in doubt. Today, some two thirds of the 2.9 billion peoples of our world are undernourished, poorly clothed, and inadequately housed, yet demographers tell us that world population will reach 6 billion souls by the end of the century.

It is among lesser developed countries, least prepared to increase food production with their traditional farming and reactionary customs, that population pressures are fast building up into a dangerous and explosive situation as they double their numbers in 25–35 years. The problems of each country stand out against a world crisis in food.

Land, the struggle for it, the fight to keep it, to live on it and wrest sufficient food and riches from it, is all-important in a world relentlessly pressed for living space and good agricultural land where populations are skyrocketing. These teeming masses of hungry peoples must be fed and clothed, or produce equivalents, from lands they now occupy, where resources are plundered or conserved, developed or undeveloped.

This doubt in civilization's race with famine is not due so much to limitations of earth's resources, as to resistance to the take-up of advanced science, technology, and works in agriculture and in developments of other resources, by about two thirds of mankind who are essentially subsistence farmers. A heavy hand of the past holds back potentialities of the present primitive societies.

Actually, we are now in a great world revolution, which may require a hundred years to stabilize a new order. It is a breakup of the age-old exploitive systems—of landlords over peasants, of rich exploiting the poor, of those with special privilege living off the backs of many. It is Colonial Governments giving freedom to colonies and protectorates, and the demand of hundreds of millions of people for human dignity and some of the good things of life.

The American people have sown seeds of social unrest throughout the world, first in the Declaration of Independence with the proposition that "all men are created equal, that they are endowed by their Creator with certain unalienable Rights, that among these are Life, Liberty and the pursuit of Happiness." Next in "government of the people, by the people, for the people," and then in the Four Freedoms of the Atlantic Charter, especially are they interested in "Freedom from Want." These great teachings have aroused hopes of mankind with spectacular force as of atomic bombs. Less developed peoples are rising to realize better conditions for themselves, usually with extravagant demands. But all too often the harvest of this social unrest is reaped by the sickle of communism.

These less developed peoples are not ready for self-government, yet they are getting it. They cannot leap overnight the centuries of struggle and discipline such as advanced countries have undergone. No one can *give* a people a culture, a progressive agriculture, or a modern civilization. They must *earn* the progress and good things they desire. But with full collaboration on their part, we can assist them to shorten the time to establish democratic and more abundant ways of life.

Land is the foundation on which nations and peoples rise or fall. If productivity is improved and maintained, peoples may grow in prosperity, providing there is social justice and freedom from aggression. If lands are damaged or devastated and farmers are exploited as is done in much of the less developed regions, then malnutrition, unrest, riots, and eventual revolution and wars are in store.

Land that grows food sustains the entire social structure and is the hope of the future. It is not an economic commodity, but is a vital part of the nation, even as its people are. Efficiency of farmers in growing food determines the number of others who may be released for various divisions of labor in a developing society. The farmer is the key to progress. His ability to double food production as populations double is all-important to the nation.

My thirty-nine years as technical assistant in agriculture, in the United States, and in countries of the Far East, Middle East and Africa, has let me observe the effects of population pressures under varying conditions.

CHINA

The Chinese make up about one fourth of the human race and three fourths of them are farmers. Much can be learned from their experiences under varying population pressures during a recorded history of 4000 years. I cannot speak for conditions under the present regime, but I spent the years 1922–27 and 1942–43 in programs of famine prevention, north of the Yangtze and west to Tibet. I learned to know firsthand the Chinese farmer and his problems and have a high regard for his splendid qualities. I know he is not communistic by choice. He is individualistic, industrious, self-reliant, intelligent, and reverent. These sturdy farmers fed the Chinese people under annual cropping of fields for forty centuries. Now they cannot grow enough food for exploding populations.

My former experiences with famines in overpopulated areas of China present a terrifying picture of what many less developed or backward countries face as populations double without a proportionate increase of food production. There is nothing more terrifying than food riots, and there is no more terrible way to reduce population than by starvation.

In famines, the frail structure of civilization falls apart. People will sell their liberty and their all for food when faced with a choice between food and starvation. A starving man knows no God and no country. I have found that hungry people do not keep their treaties, neither will they keep the peace, nor will they stay within their own boundaries. Hunger and poverty are the enemies of liberty and breed totalitarianism and communism. There is no substitute for food.

AFRICA, SOUTH OF THE SAHARA

Today, the eyes of the world are on Africa as never before. Africa, with its vast resources, harbors forces of instability that may affect the peace of the world. Millions of people, unlearned and unskilled, are being given freedom and self-govenment. In past years the white man in Africa generally failed to train the African in fundamental skills for economic independence or to demonstrate the dignity of labor.

While serving as consultant to the British Colonial Office and to missions in Africa, I spoke to many thousands of African students in high school and junior college assemblies. In each place I asked for a showing of hands of those who were training for different lines of work. Many were preparing to be clerks or schoolteachers, some to be lawyers, doctors, and politicians. Not one of these thousands announced that he was preparing to be a skilled mechanic, and none to be mechanical, civil, electrical, or agricultural engineers or modern farmers. I said, "Now you want self-government, but no one of you is preparing to carry on the basic and productive works of a self-governing state."

As these new states attain self-government, they are finding that they lack trained personnel for productive enterprises and are frantically calling for technical assistance from the United Nations or from whatever country will supply experts. A most urgent problem is to step up production of foodstuffs sufficient for rapidly increasing populations from lands badly damaged and deteriorating under primitive farming. Difficulties are not only scientific and technical but include resistance of traditional farmers. For the heavy hand of the past strikes fear in the illiterate masses and hangs heavy over all farming operations. It crushes individual initiative, the greatest asset of a nation. Native agriculture, as it is practiced, is not keeping and cannot keep pace with the increasing numbers.

Present leaders in Africa, ambitious to establish prosperous new nations, face tremendous problems in overcoming deep-seated resistance of farmers to adopt improved conservation farming. Old-fashioned African chiefs, with few exceptions, have been a powerful reactionary force with arbitrary powers, especially in customs controlling the tenure of tribal land. Chiefs suspect educated Africans and fear any competitor in leadership.

African farmers live from day to day and crop to crop. They eat when they have food and starve when they do not. They give little thought to being provident for the future; if they have a surplus, others would likely take it from them or live with them as long as it lasts. Colonial governments helped certain farmers carry out demonstration plots with composting, fertilizers, improved seeds, and with soil conservation, beside plots of traditional farming which increased production manyfold. But few if any farmers carried out these practices on their own initiative, and they dropped the demonstration plots immediately when white supervision was removed. As colonial administrations come to an end, only time will reveal what progress the African will make to increase food production.

Millions of people, living in tropical Africa, the "hothouse" of the world, practice an early Iron Age agriculture. Vast regions have not reached the plow stage. Farmers practice "shifting cultivation" wherein they use fire as a tool, along with a stubby ax and a shorthandled hoe, and move to a new patch of "bush" after two or three crops. But now population pressure has reduced the former cycle of twenty years until in many localities farmers must cultivate the same impoverished ground, year after year.

Technical problems for development of the vast resources of Africa are more easily solved than human, including debilitating diseases. African people are not prepared to develop their resources or accept the rapid change necessary and accept the challenge of programs of training in many specialties from labor forces, skilled artisans, scientists, technologists, doctors, and administrators for many installations and works.

With energetic programs and skilled people, Africa can be made to supply local needs in a more prosperous society and export sufficient to supply all Europe with such products as rice, paper pulp, palm and peanut oils, cocoa, tropical fruits, cabinet woods, rubber, tobacco, copper, iron, chrome, diamonds, and other things in quantity. It is a pity that in the midst of such potentialities, I found people undernourished, sometimes suffering famine, yet resisting progress.

INDIA

India demonstrates on a tremendous scale how hard it is to step up production of foodstuffs and other agricultural crops when a population of over 400 million, rapidly increasing, has already reduced farm units to such small areas as to grow little more than subsistence for the farm family, still leaving many landless. Here the farmer can produce little or no surplus to feed other divisions of society or to give him purchasing power to buy other good things he craves. His farming cannot meet the oncoming crisis except by drastic measures.

Now, the prospects are that the great efforts of government to help farmers grow more food will serve only to give the increasing millions of the country no more food than the present inadequate diet. It is predicted that at best, India at the end of the third five-year plan will face an alarming food deficit.

India is having to face up to this problem on a large scale which the world is facing in varying degrees in different regions. This is a vital challenge that overrides the niceties of economic equations. These are the horrifying facts of life on this planet.

NORTH AFRICA AND THE MIDDLE EAST

These old lands, which once sustained large and prosperous populations and many glorious Roman cities, ruins of which amaze archaeologists and tourists, are now occupied by sparse populations of Arab peoples with very low economic standards of living. This is a sorry commentary on man's plunder of the "Good Earth" which bequeathed to peoples of this century, with their increasing demands, "man-made deserts" of overgrazed, deforested, eroded lands, malarial swamps, and marching sand dunes.

I have traveled some 26,000 miles in overland surveys throughout these lands, except Saudi Arabia and Yemen, and have seen firsthand their problems. These are not lack of land, or overpopulation, except in Egypt, but rather are social, economical, and political.

For twelve centuries, peoples of North Africa and the Middle East suffered a long decline due to invasions, wars, ruinous taxation, exploitation by landlords of peasants, soil erosion, neglect of land, and overgrazing by ubiquitous goats, beginning with the first Arab invasion in 640 A.D. Nowhere has the interrelation between deterioration of land and privations of peoples been so clear as here.

Landlordism is deeply entrenched. Landlords resist efforts to break down their age-old racket of exploiting peasants. They have not yet shown a social consciousness to improve the lot of workers. Today there is much talk, but despite the white light of publicity and work of international agencies, there is little social justice for oppressed peasants. Furthermore, a lethargy prevails due to the dictum that "what is, is the will of Allah." Land reform moves slowly and leaves many peasants still oppressed and exploited in Moslem lands.

However, the French in North Africa and the Israelis in the Middle East have demonstrated remarkable ways in which these deteriorated Roman lands may be rejuvenated with vision, hard work, science, technology, and measures of modern conservation.

The French have restored and extended irrigation and plantations of olive trees and vineyards. They reclaimed marshes and irrigated dry lands, built dams for reservoirs, built tens of thousands of miles of banquettes or terraces on eroding hills of Arabs and Berbers, planting them to orchards and vineyards and increasing land values fifteenfold. Better nutrition, medical services, and sanitation let Arab populations double in twenty years. Since 50 percent are now under twenty years of age, coming reproductive years will bring on a population explosion.

ISRAEL

Israelis, since Independence in 1948, have done remarkable works that have meaning as a pilot project for the Middle East and for much of the world where population presses on the land. For Israel more than doubled her population in ten years, while accomplishing a twofold task, rehabilitating a million destitute immigrants and reclaiming a man-made desert.

IRAQ

Iraq, or ancient Mesopotamia, is the greatest unused and undeveloped "breadbasket" of the world today. Ancient Babylon here had an estimated 20 million population in a powerful empire, as compared to 5–6 million today in a general state of illiteracy and poverty. The rich alluvial valleys of the Tigris-Euphrates and their lifegiving waters are still there to support, under modern agriculture and technology, eight to ten times the present population, and with a much higher standard of living. There is a population and labor vacuum in the lands of Iraq and northern Syria that requires immigration of skilled farmers and technologists to create once more a prosperous country.

EGYPT

Egypt presents a special case. It contains the richest land on earth and the poorest farmers. Exploitation by landlords, overpopulation, malnutrition, and disease plague this country. The government is now attempting to reduce size of holdings available to landed gentry and to industrialize. Moreover, the great Aswan Dam is expected to irrigate 1.7 million acres of new land. But by the time this Aswan project is completed, increase of population will about eat up increases in production. Drawbacks are that it will inundate 50,000 acres of excellent cultivated land, the city of Khartoum, priceless antiquities, and will expose a vast surface of water in the driest and hottest part of the world where 30 percent will be lost by evaporation.

But the engineered "Century Storage Plan" calling for collaboration of four countries offers far greater benefits. Storage to increase and equalize flow of the Nile through a century would be gained in the great lakes of Central Africa where rainfall exceeds evaporation, by raising outlets of lakes such as is being done at Owens Falls of Lake Victoria. Hydropower and irrigation waters would be increased, providing security for production of crops throughout the Nile Valley. Growth of populations challenges nations to collaborate in full development of natural resources to gain more abundance for all peoples concerned.

Birth control to limit populations is a touchy matter across international boundaries. At an International Conference in Israel in 1960, representatives of Afro-Asian states rejected such a suggestion as a "trick of white men to keep down black populations." "No," they said emphatically, "we want to increase our populations rapidly to become strong, with a voice in world affairs." This touchy problem can only be handled by the country concerned, as Japan is doing.

This oncoming population explosion must also stimulate foresight and collaboration among nations, individually and collectively, through international efforts, in development of works worthy of the human spirit. This calls for productive economies that enable peoples to *earn* security in good things of life. This is a challenge greater than war and would cost burdened taxpayers less. In my view, the potentialities of the "Good Earth" are so great, under the new and enlarged powers that the modern scientific and technological revolution puts into our hands, that we have a fighting chance to win this race with famine.

MAHOMMEDALI C. CHAGLA, former Indian Ambassador to the United States, is a member of a three-man commission to investigate Sikh discrimination in India. Chagla received his education at Lincoln College, Oxford, and since 1947 has been Vice-Chancellor of Bombay University and Chief Justice of the Bombay High Court.

India's Dilemma

M. C. CHAGLA

There is no more vital issue facing the world than that of increasing population. We are so engrossed in piling up armaments either to unleash an atomic war or to defend ourselves against one that we are apt to forget or overlook the terrible menace that is threatening the world—the menace of rising expectations with a growing population which can never hope to satisfy these expectations.

This century has seen the practical liquidation of colonialism and the emergence of new and independent countries in Asia and Africa. Practically all these countries were underdeveloped. A colonial economy forced them to be the suppliers of raw materials to be manufactured by the colonizing countries and sent back to the colonies for the consumption of their people. The majority of the population lived on a level of bare subsistence. There was vast illiteracy, chronic unemployment, hunger and disease were rampant, and there was a fatalistic resignation to a fate from which nothing better or higher could be expected. In the beginning of the twentieth-century, empires and colonies, developed and underdeveloped countries, affluent and poor societies were accepted as the law of nature which nothing could or should alter.

The two world wars shook political and economic thinking to its foundations. Politically every nation was conceded the right of self-determination. Economically every country which became free claimed the right to raise the standard of living of its people so as at least to approximate if not to equal that of the richer communities.

The first revolution that was achieved in these newly independent countries was a striking improvement in the health of the people. It was comparatively cheap and easy to abolish epidemics, to check infant mortality and to raise the expectancy of life. In India the expectancy of life has gone up from about 20 in 1930 to 42 today. The death rate has gone down from 30 per thousand to 20 per thousand. These are impressive figures of which our country is justifiably proud. But this is only one side of the picture. This is the picture of what advancing civilization can do, bringing in its train research in medicine and surgery, better methods of prevention of disease and sanitation. But civilization has also inflicted a terrible injury upon society. It has interfered with ways of nature or Providence in increasing life and preventing early deaths. It has fought pestilence and disease. Politically, by maintaining a stable government we have done away with local wars, which accounted for losses of thousands of lives. The result has been a steadily increasing population. Our population in 1911 was 250 million. In 1951 it was 351 million. In the census just taken it has reached 438 million, an increase of about 25 percent in ten years. What do these figures portend? A dark and dismal future for millions, bitterness and frustration, poverty and unemployment, political discontent and unrest.

Since our independence in 1947 we have made a striking advance on almost all fronts—education, agriculture, industry, and village upliftment. We have just prepared our third Five Year Plan in which these advances would be maintained and even accelerated. We hope to transform a backward, purely agricultural economy into a prosperous and industrial one. We had planned on the basis of our population in 1961 being 430 million. This increase of 8 million increases our almost intolerable burden a hundredfold. We have to find food, education, and employment for these 8 million additional people.

In India, as in other countries similarly situated, civilization must advance on two fronts. It would lead to a terrible imbalance if the advance is maintained and pressed only on one front. This imbalance would be a potential source not only of holding down the progress of the country, but might result in political and economic instability and even chaos. The one front I have already dealt with—improving the health of the people, looking after the welfare of children, improving the sanitation in villages. But the other front should not be neglected—population control and family planning. Our government has not been oblivious or neglectful of the vital importance of this front. It realizes that India's future is bound up with the question of the pressure of population.

We have done something which few governments have had the courage to do. In a highly religious country we have officially adopted the policy of family planning and the government has taken steps to give effect to that policy. I need hardly say that orthodox religions all over the

world take up the same unconvincing attitude toward
birth control, that it is an interference with the unscrutable
ways of God and we must leave it to Him to look after
those whom He brings into this world. It is forgotten that
every new discovery for combating disease is as much an
interference with the limit of life set by Providence, and
with regard to the second argument it is an insult to the
goodness of God to suggest that He has ordained that
children should be born into poverty and destitution and
should have not even a ray of hope to better their conditions.
We are fortunate in India that religious opposition
has not been vocal or vociferous.

Two conditions must be satisfied before any program
for birth control can be successfully carried out. The government
must put everything it has behind such a program—all
its drive and energy. It must give it top priority.
It must realize that everything it does in the way of improving
agriculture and industry would be like writing on
the sand—the massive waves of increasing population
would wipe it out. Let us see what our government has
already done. It has provided 52 million dollars for family
planning in the third Five Year Plan as against 10 million
dollars in the second plan. In 1956 there were 147 birth
control clinics; today there are about 3000. The sale of
contraceptives has gone up six times from 1956 to 1958
and most of them are supplied free. But this is still too
little. We are facing a volcanic eruption, and all the methods
known to science, all the propaganda that public-spirited
citizens are capable of, all the money that could
possibly be spared must be utilized in this cause. If we
can check our population it would make all the difference
between poverty and plenty, between a contented society

and a society that has been driven to choose undemocratic methods to try and solve what seems to be an almost insoluble problem.

I think the second condition can be easily satisfied. I am convinced that people here, especially the women, are willing to cooperate in any planned drive for birth control or family planning. At one time people wanted a large family as an insurance, since so few children survived. Now a large family actually means a large family, with all the headaches and heartaches which it implies. The poor people—and that means an overwhelming majority of the country—want to be shown some simple and cheap method of controlling their family. The best evidence of this comes from the success so drastic a remedy as sterilization is achieving. There were 7823 sterilizations in 1956; in 1960 there were 41,091. The hospitals in many Indian states have been instructed to perform the operation, which is simple, painless, and free. A person must have at least three children before he can take this irrevocable step. More and more people are resorting to this sure way out of an intolerable situation.

Ultimately any country can only succeed in achieving its objective by its own effort and determination. But our problem is so herculean that we need the help of the world outside. Not monetary help, but the help that comes from a roused conscience which feels the same urgency of fighting this fell disease, because it is a sickness from which mankind is suffering as it does with regard to cancer or a thousand and one other ailments to which human flesh is heir.

CHIKAO HONDA graduated from Waseda University, Tokyo, in 1920 and went into newspaper work. In 1945 he was made editor-in-chief of the Osaka Mainichi newspapers and in 1948 was appointed president. He is now chairman of the Population Problems Research Council in Tokyo.

Japan's Solution

CHIKAO HONDA

Not until the "rice riot" shook Japan in 1918 and not until the first population census in the modern sense of the word was taken there in 1920, did the Japanese become conscious of and feel a real challenge in the population problem.

In 1894 Dr. Hiroyuki Kato, a noted Malthusian scholar, warned the nation against the dangers of coming over-population, but nobody paid much attention to him.

During the period of about 140 years prior to the Restoration era of Meiji, which started in 1868, Japan's population was stagnant at the level of about 32 million. But with the dawn of the Restoration, followed by an industrial revolution which actually began around 1890, the picture began to change. The industrial revolution caused a rapid increase in population, which in turn became one of the important factors in furthering the industrial revolution itself.

The "rice riot" of 1918, caused by a sharp rise in the price of rice, which is the staple food for the Japanese people, became a vital topic of national controversy. It was understood generally at that time that the broken balance between population growth and increase of food production was a population problem. A heated controversy between the Malthusian and Marxian theories on population among leading experts drew wide attention. The Japanese government in 1925 established the Population and Food Problems Research Council in an attempt to cope with the situation.

The 1920 census revealed that the population of Japan at that time was 55.4 million, which meant an increase of 1.6 times during the period of forty-eight years since 1872, the year when the government first undertook a population count throughout the nation.

Japan today has a population of 93,418,501 according to the National Census conducted in October 1960, which is an increase of 4.6 percent in the last five years. This huge population is now forced to live in an area about the same size as the state of Montana in the United States.

In 1945 when World War II ended, Japan's population was less than 72 million. During several years after the war ended, more than 6.3 million Japanese military servicemen and civilian evacuees, mostly young people, were repatriated from overseas, causing an unusually big increase in the nation's population. Despite a substantial decline of fertility in recent years, the rate of average annual increase still maintains on the level of more than one percent of the total population.

In prewar years, the rate of natural increase of the nation's population reached the peak around 1930 when its capitalistic economy entered its prime.

An obvious decline in the rate of population increase

in Japan was first observed toward the end of World War II. However, a remarkable increase soon followed and nearly 55 percent of the subsequent 20 million increase took place during the period from 1945 to 1950.

In demographers' analyses, such surprising increase in postwar years was attributed to: 1) a social increase caused by repatriation of military personnel and civilian evacuees from overseas; 2) the so-called "baby boom" that lasted from 1947 to 1949, which recorded 34.4 births per 1000 population; 3) a notable decline of mortality, due to the marked improvement in medical and sanitary techniques.

Hard pressed by the rapid increase in the population, Japan had to deal with it by her own efforts. And she did it with a noticeable success.

An epoch was made in the nation's birth control movement in 1948 when the Japanese Diet passed the Eugenic Protection Law to permit induced abortion and sterilization. Since then the number of induced abortions increased year after year until 1955 when a total of 1,170,000 cases were officially registered. This was about five times as many as the figures for 1949.

Birth control, the practice of contraception in particular, was now widely recognized by the populace, due to big efforts by both the government and private organizations. The government has assigned a large number of health officials and maternity nurses to give people technical advice through circuit lectures and distribution of free medicines and instruments.

Despite the postwar baby boom in Japan, the birth rate has steadily declined, due to a planned parenthood movement. According to official statistics, the birth rate in 1959 registered 17.55—nearly half of the rate in 1947, the year it hit the postwar peak.

The rate of natural increase in population—births minus deaths—dropped in 1957 to 8.87 per 1000 persons from the 21.63 in 1948. This was the lowest ever recorded in Japan's modern demography, and was also observed as a spectacular phenomenon by demographic specialists the world over.

The surprising decline of birth rate in Japan in recent years was unparalleled among the countries of the world. It is called a "miracle of Japan's population."

It must be noted, however, that the birth rate in Japan has again been showing a slight increase since 1958, along with the increase in marriages, reflecting to some extent the improved economic life of the Japanese people. But most observers do believe that the birth rate will not return to the prewar level and that the present rate will remain more or less stationary for a long time to come, for the reasons explained below.

The field surveys conducted by the Mainichi Newspapers' Population Problems Research Council since 1950 indicate that individual Japanese families are anxious to keep their size small. The surveys show that the people's desire for a small family is becoming stronger yearly and that the majority of returns to the survey were in favor of restricting the number of children to less than two.

It is an important fact to observe that the economic boom in Japan today owes much to the efforts of the people in general to rationalize and modernize their family life on the basis of planned parenthood. This way of thinking is closely related to the collapse of the conventional family system in Japan, which has taken place parallel to the democratization of Japanese community life.

In 1959 couples who had practiced or were practicing contraception in one way or another represented 57 percent of the total families included in the survey. The survey also indicated that the economic difficulty of maintaining a large-size family is the most important factor for diffusion of contraception. Other factors in order of preference were "consideration of mother's health," "desire to enjoy life," and what not.

It is a good sign for the future of planned parenthood in Japan that induced abortion, as a means to limit births, has been visibly replaced by contraception because of the possibility of injury to mothers' health and public morals.

Among several important features of Japan's population problems, it should be recognized that the nation's population is still young, due to the phenomenal rise of the birth rate in postwar years, which makes an interesting comparison with the age distribution in England, France, and other European countries.

However, as the result of the declining birth rate in recent years, the percentage of children under the age of fifteen is diminishing, while the productive-age population, between fifteen and sixty-four, and the aged population between sixty-five and over, show a gradual increase. Demographers estimate that the productive-age population will increase by nearly 12 million in the next decade, while the total population will increase by 6 million in the same period. The aged population is estimated to increase by about 1.6 million during the same period, while children under the age of fifteen will decrease by 6.9 million.

Such being the case, the declining child population will have to sustain a heavier population pressure from older people for some years after they grow up into productive ages. Thus, the age distribution of Japan's population implies the foremost demographic problem—a fundamental issue for future economic planning.

The constant decrease in the birth rate since 1950 has been causing the proportion of children in the population of Japan to shrink and that of the productive-age population to rise to a considerable extent, resulting in a sharp aging of the entire population.

As to the aged population, experts believe that it will reach the level of 10 million by 1990 and even thereafter it will continue to increase by about 2 million a year for at least thirty years to come if the present mortality rate remains to continue.

Another important feature of Japan's population movement is the concentration of population in urban areas. The latest census shows that Japan's population increased by 5,900,000 during the five-year period from 1950 to 1955. Nearly 70 percent of the increase was recorded in six prefectures where six large cities including Tokyo and Osaka are located.

On the other hand, the increase in rural population which supplies industrial areas with labor force has been very slow. In some rural districts, the rate of "social decrease" has surpassed the rate of natural increase, resulting in the relative decrease of population.

Coping with such concentration of population in urban areas is an important problem for city planners and employment officials. The situation is very serious in Tokyo, where a very large number of rural inhabitants are coming in annually, mostly to seek jobs and better wages.

Urban areas provide relatively abundant opportunities for jobs, higher education, and wider choice of amusement, all of which naturally attract more people from rural communities. But the main factor for the migration of rural population into urban areas is the teeming population pressure in rural communities, particularly in agricultural communities where the rising agricultural productivity is bringing about more surplus labor.

In spite of some remarkable achievements made so far by Japan to cope with the nation's population problems, we all realize that there is no panacea, no sudden remedy, and there lies the principal difficulty.

The problems Japan faces today can be summarized as: 1) the problem of regulating the nation's births to keep them at a low rate; 2) the problem of finding employment for the fast-increasing productive-age group; 3) the problem of finding measures for the maintenance of the growing aged population.

Thanks to the prevalence of the planned parenthood movement, the birth rate in Japan has declined since the postwar "baby boom." However, Japan's economy is going to face a serious dilemma in the next ten years, when the productive-age population is expected to increase greatly.

The urgent need is for Japanese industries to rationalize their structural production to enable them to raise productivity and compete with foreign products in world markets, for Japan can survive only through sufficient export. At the same time, it can be assumed that rationalization of structural production, as it progresses, would eventually bring about surplus labor and lessen the possibility of full employment for the teeming productive-age population.

Under these circumstances, Japan's economy should fulfill the following three requirements simultaneously: 1) new employment opportunities to absorb at a higher rate than before, the currently increasing labor population; 2) modernization of industrial and employment structures by reforming those enterprises which are being operated under an obsolete system of management; 3) increase of employment and raising of per capita income through the improvement of productivity.

In recent years Japan's economic growth has been registering a rate of more than 7.5 percent in gross national production per annum. Even under such favorable circumstances, it will be extremely difficult for the nation's economy to fulfill all the foregoing requirements.

To cope with the situation arising out of the urban concentration of population, the central and provincial governments are carrying out various projects, including the land-development program, the "capital-zone reconstruction plan" in Tokyo, and city plannings in other cities and towns.

On the whole, Japan is doing everything possible in its own power. We realize our goal is far, far ahead, but we are constantly working hard with full determination to lessen the pressure of the overpopulation and decrease the population growth.

Enrique Beltran is professor of zoology in the National University of Mexico and chief of the Laboratory of Protozoology of the Institute of Public Health and Tropical Diseases. He is permanent secretary of the Mexican Society of Natural History as well as editor of the *Review of the Institute of Public Health and Tropical Diseases*. Dr. Beltran is a member of the National Association of Biology Teachers of the United States and has taken an active interest in improving all phases of biology teaching in Mexico, especially in secondary schools.

Latin America's Prospects

ENRIQUE BELTRAN

"A moderate number of human beings can
be treated as individuals; an immense
number can be treated only in crowds."
                                    P.E.P., 1955[1]

A recent study[2] estimated Latin America's population at
approximately 154 million, not including Puerto Rico with
2.2 million inhabitants, and the estimate was considered
to fall about 2 percent short of the actual figure. If we add
Puerto Rico, undeniably Latin in its people and culture,
and if we allow for the above-mentioned adjustment, we
can assume that the population of that part of the western
hemisphere known as Latin America was about 160 million inhabitants. Since these totals date from 1950, the
author feels that by now the population will have passed
200 million.

United Nations experts in a similar study[3] calculated
the combined population of Mexico, Central and South
America (Latin America) at 162 million inhabitants, and

they estimated that by the year 2000 it would have reached 280 million, an increase of 73 percent during the half century under examination. In order to appreciate the magnitude of this figure, it must be realized that the growth of world population during the same period (from 2400 to 3250 million) would be only 55 percent. Therefore, this part of the world must be a matter of grave concern as regards the future significance of its present and expanding population pressure.

The problem is a serious one all over Latin America, but it differs sharply from one country to another, due to such circumstances as population densities which vary from 589.6 inhabitants per square mile in Puerto Rico and 289.1 in Haiti, to barely 4.9 in Bolivia and 8.5 in Paraguay. And the problem is made still more complex by the fact that high population densities are not necessarily accompanied by abundant natural resources, nor is there any correlation between population density and the recent rate of population increase. Although it is true that Bolivia, which has the lowest population density, also had the lowest rate of growth in the 1940–1950 period (4.0 percent), Peru, with a population density considerably lower than those of Puerto Rico and Haiti, nonetheless had the largest increase in population during this same period. Peru's 37.3 percent rate of increase is immediately followed by the 35.7 percent rate of Venezuela, which has a population density of 14.3 inhabitants per square mile, only slightly higher than that of Paraguay.[2]

In 1954 Echeverria[4] considered Latin America as lowly populated, because its territory is 15 percent of the world's area and its population only 7 percent of the total. But already in 1948 Vogt[5] stated that, with the exception of three or four countries, all Latin America must be considered overpopulated, taking into account not only the total number of inhabitants and population density per unit of area, but also their relation to available natural resources. These countries are threatened with biological bankruptcy, since they must meet the needs of their peoples by an accelerated destruction of their resources.

We have quoted a few figures on population and some growth projections in order to show how dramatic the problem is and how each reexamination finds it becoming increasingly acute. In fact, we have mentioned above an estimate made by the United Nations in 1951[3] for the growth of world population which must be disquieting to anyone who is not either foolishly optimistic or criminally indifferent. And only three years later, in 1954, the same United Nations experts[6] were to revise their calculations upward.

Actually, we are not too worried about the accuracy of the figures or how realistic the projections may be. In fact, reviewing the opinions of various specialists as to the maximum population the earth can support, it is immaterial whether we accept East's estimate[7] of 5200 million, given the present diet of rural Europe; Pearson and Harper's estimate,[8] which fluctuates from 2800 million by Asiatic standards to only 900 million by North American; or even Wagemann's optimistic estimate,[9] which he himself seems to mistrust, of a possible 30,000 million.

These different estimates, together with associated ones regarding the rate of growth of resources, only mean advancing or postponing the inevitable moment when the earth can no longer support more inhabitants and when *Standing Room Only*, the grim title of Sax's thoughtful and well-documented book,[10] will have become a reality.

And to reach these limits, which may appear fantastic, it is not necessary to assume an annual growth of 2.9 percent such as Mexico had between 1953 and 1957,[11] or even the higher ones of other Latin American countries. It suffices to mention Durand's reference[12] to the Argentine demographer following the absurd biblical estimate of a human past of 7000 years (which we now know to be about 500,000) who says that if Adam and Eve and their descendants had had a compound growth of one percent there would be so many human beings in the world today that, standing back to back, they would cover the surface of a sphere with a circumference equal to fourteen times the orbit of Neptune.

It is true that not all the world is uniformly populated, and thus large-scale migrations might momentarily relieve an exceptional pressure in a given area. It is also true that advances in science and technology have shown the way to increase the production of foodstuffs and other materials necessary to our existence. But neither the improved distribution of population nor the increase in productivity may be considered definitive remedies, but only palliatives.

The majority of mankind is still undernourished, in spite of the unquestionable and at times marvelous progress made in food production during the last century. Why do we persist in this mad race of population increase against an increase in the means of subsistence? Would it not be more rational and, above all, more human to try to restrain such an explosive increase in population, and at the same time to try to promote the production of foodstuffs and other materials? Thus, instead of wildly gambling with future possibilities, we would daily raise human living standards.

Those future possibilities of productive development are sometimes very optimistic, but careful consideration frequently shows that there are no solid grounds for such an attitude.

Taking Mexico as an example of Latin America's conditions, we may easily realize how different limiting factors put boundaries to an unrestricted population growth. The country area is, in round figures, 2,000,000 square kilometers, and the population—according to preliminary estimates of 1960 Census—over 35 million, giving a population density of 17.5 inhabitants per square kilometer.

The mountainous character of the country is a fundamental limit to future agricultural development because of the reduced extension of level lands proper for cultivation. But still more important is the fact that most of the country has neither enough nor well-balanced rainfall to insure regular crops.

According to some recent estimates,[13] about 94 percent of the Mexican territory may be classified as arid or semiarid, where irrigation is necessary. That means about 188,-000,000 hectares (a hectare is equal to 2.471 acres), which may be put under sound production only if they are irrigated and suitably level.

Starting in 1926, all Mexican governments have paid a great deal of attention to irrigation programs, and to the end of 1958 it was estimated that the total investment in such programs was $11,717,500,000 (Mexican currency, figured in the value of the peso at this moment) or the equivalent of $934,400,000. And only 2,238,810 hectares were irrigated.

Garcia Quintero[14] figures the maximum possibilities for irrigation in Mexico in the arid and semiarid zones, utilizing all available waters, as only a little less than 13 million hectares. Furthermore, including the possibilities of the remaining 6 percent of the territory classified as semihumid or humid, the total extension with available water could only reach a maximum of about 17.5 million hectares. Considering a 1980 population of 60 million people —which is not the highest possible estimate—the land area with sure water for agriculture should be of the order of 0.3 hectare per inhabitant.

This estimate is not very encouraging but it is still optimistic because, taking into consideration the total area irrigated from 1926 to 1958 as being only 2.2 millon hectares, it is quite unlikely that in the next twenty years it could be possible to increase this amount in the order required to use all available water possibilities.

If we remember that many other Latin American countries like Colombia, Venezuela, Brazil, Peru, Bolivia, Paraguay, Chile, and Argentina also have extensive arid zones, it is possible to visualize the handicap such conditions represent in regard to future population increases.

The limiting factor represented by arid lands is generally admitted and need not be emphasized, although quite frequently it is dismissed on the assumption that human action, through irrigation, will correct the situation and convert such arid zones into highly productive areas. As we have seen with the Mexican example, this is not true, because available water—on the surface or underground —is also limited in many places.

But most people think that the humid tropics in Latin

America, covered by luxuriant jungle, hold unlimited possibilities for the future. Such optimists think only sanitation and colonization of those low-populated areas are needed to convert them into highly productive lands.

Unfortunately in most cases, that is not true, not only because of the costly drainage programs required in many of such areas to dispose of excess water, but also on account of poor soil conditions.

We find both limiting factors in a recent and extensive study of the humid, tropical southeast Mexico.[15] It is mostly level land and has abundant rainfall, and the conjugation of these two favorable factors has led many to consider it as an area of unlimited agricultural possibilities. But the very thin and unsuitable soil in most of the area will not permit any sound agriculture there.

The research done in the great Amazon basin, on which high hopes were formerly centered, has produced the same results as in southeast Mexico.

That is why we agree with Price[16] when he says: "The old theory that the hot, wet tropics, with their dense vegetation are almost wholly of great fertility, is incorrect, for it is clear that the tropics include many sterile soils."

If Latin American countries, in general, conjugate a very high rate of population increase with serious limiting factors in the actual and potential use of available natural resources of the area, it is clear that the old view still prevailing in many groups, based on the desirability of promoting population growth to increase productivity, is quite misleading and may easily breed disaster.

If an improvement in man's future is contemplated, rational birth planning is not an absolute remedy unless it takes into account other important aspects. Nevertheless, we feel that Frederick Osborn[17] is correct in his belief that a change in the social structure to smaller families as a result of deliberate planning would lead to the adoption of other constructive measures.

Unfortunately, the adoption of rational measures to limit the birth rate meets with the opposition of powerful social groups, especially in the case of Latin America, where the Roman Catholic Church raises its voice against any human effort to interfere with the bringing of new lives into the world.

And although it is possible to accept Meier's comment,[18] based on investigations carried out in Jamaica, that ". . . the individual acceptance of birth control is not substantially reduced if the potential users are of Catholic persuasion," it is clear that the existence of an active and organized opposition, such as that of the Roman Church, represents an enormous obstacle.

We believe that most of the preceding considerations are valid for the entire world, since the problem of unlimited population growth is universal and, although less apparent, possibly in the long run a more certain threat to the survival of our species than the most dreadful nuclear weapon imaginable.

We think it is urgent to define the problem, and if remedies are to be applied and one of them is birth control, it is also urgent to combat those who are in opposition.

"If we evade the choice, the inevitable looms ahead of us—even sterner forces will make the decision for us. We cannot delay or evade. For now, as we look, we can see the limits of the earth." (Fairfield Osborn)[19]

REFERENCES

1. Political & Economic Planning. *World Population and Resources.* London: George Allen and Unwin, 1955; Fair Lawn, N. J.: Essential Books, 1955.

2. Smith, T. Lynn. *Latin American Population Studies.* Social Sciences No. 8, University of Florida Monographs, 1960.

3. United Nations Dept. of Social Affairs. *The Past and Future Growth of World Population—A Long Range View.* Population Bulletin No. 1, December 1951.

4. Echeverria, L. M. *Geografía Humana,* Mexico, 1954.

5. Vogt, William. *Road to Survival.* New York: William Sloane Associates, 1948.

6. United Nations Dept. of Social Affairs. *Framework for Future Population Estimates, 1950–1980, by World Regions.* Mimeograph, 1954.

7. East, Edward M. *Mankind at the Crossroads.* New York: Charles Scribner's Sons, 1923.

8. Pearson, Frank A. and Harper, Floyd A. *The World's Hunger.* Ithaca, N. Y.: Cornell University Press, 1945.

9. Wagemann, E. F. *Menschenzahl and Völkerschicksal,* Hamburg, 1948.

10. Sax, Karl. *Standing Room Only: The Challenge of Overpopulation.* Boston: Beacon Press, 1955.

11. Loyo, G. "La Poblacion de Mexico," *Mesas Redondas sobre los Recursos Naturales y el Crecimiento Demografico de Mexico,* Instituto Mexicana de Recoursas Naturales Renovables, Mexico, 1960.

12. Durand, J. D. "World Population: Trend and Prospects." In *Population and World Politics,* edited by Philip M. Hauser. Glencoe, Ill.: The Free Press of Glencoe, 1958.

13. Orive Alba, A. *La Politica de Irrigacion en Mexico,* Mexico, 1960.

14. Garcia Quintero, A. cited by A. Rodriguez L. in *Mesas Redondas sobre los Recursos Naturales y el Crecimiento Demografico de Mexico,* Instituto Mexicana de Recoursas Naturales Renovables, Mexico, 1959.

15. Beltran, E. *Los Recursos Naturales del Sureste y su Aprovechamiento,* Mexico, 1959.

16. Price, A. G. *White Settlers in the Tropics*. New York: American Geographical Society of New York, 1939.

17. Osborn, Frederick. *Population: An International Dilemma*. New York: Population Council, 1958.

18. Meier, Richard L. *Modern Science and the Human Fertility Problem*. New York: John Wiley & Sons, 1959.

19. Osborn, Fairfield. *The Limits of the Earth*. Boston: Little, Brown & Co., 1953.

PART IV

The Population Problem
and Religion

FATHER ROBERT I. GANNON, former President of Fordham University, graduated from Georgetown University in 1913, entered the Society of Jesus and went to Woodstock College for his M.A. He was ordained priest in 1926, received an S.T.D. degree from the Gregorian University in Rome (1927), and an M.A. from Christ's College, Cambridge University (1930). He is the recipient of many honorary degrees. Father Gannon was Dean of St. Peter's College from 1930 to 1936 and then President of Fordham University until 1949, when he was appointed Director of the Jesuit Retreat Home at Manresa, Staten Island. Father Gannon is the author of four books: *The Technique of the One-Act Play, After Black Coffee* (a collection of his afterdinner speeches), *Poor Old Liberal Arts,* and *The Cardinal Spellman Story.* He is a member of many organizations, including the New York Zoological Society.

A Roman Catholic Speaks

THE REV. ROBERT I. GANNON

There is a monolithic illusion about Roman Catholic attitudes even among otherwise informed observers. Because the old Church is definite and immutable when it deals with the essentials of Faith and morals, there is a tendency to regard it as fixed in its views on every subject down to the smallest detail. On closer inspection, outsiders are often amazed at the differences of opinion they find in Rome, not only in scientific and philosophical matters, but even in theological as well.

So with the question of "Population Pressures and the Roman Catholic Church." The answer cannot be wrapped up and delivered in a word like Calvin Coolidge's famous sermon on sin. The Church is not for overpopulation or against control. The fact is that there is no peculiarly Roman Catholic viewpoint with regard to this recognized crisis. On many details concerning the problems that are arising from it and the various proposed solutions offered, there is as much difference of opinion among Catholics as among the members of any other group, and where Cath-

187

olics are unanimous, as they are on certain well-known moral aspects of control, their conviction is shared by at least some sections of their non-Catholic neighbors.

There are all sorts of people of every religion and of no religion who refuse to take the whole situation seriously. Some like to remind themselves of the miscalculations of the Reverend Thomas Malthus on England's future, and when anyone begins an exposition with the words "if the present trend continues," they smile and bring up the case of the little boy who made one dollar the first week and two the second. If the trend had continued, his income in half a year would have been over a million a week! Others in their laudable veneration for Divine Providence minimize man's role of cooperation. They never worry about current or future events. It is all part of God's plan and He has all the answers which He can give us in His own good time. The more self-centered may admit that something should be done, but not by them. They are not their brother's keepers and happen to have plenty of elbow room at the moment in South Dakota. No one has told them that overpopulation just means "too many consumers for available supplies" and can be absolute, applying to all mankind, or relative, applying to certain parts of the race at certain times. They take it for granted that the main problem is concerned with absolute overpopulation —the intriguing prospect of standing room only on the earth in seven hundred years! So, like many people who are not at all selfish, they resent hearing from one set of alarmists that there may not be any human race by Christmas, and from another set, that in the foreseeable future there may not be space left for a tennis court, let alone a golf course, in America.

Many Catholics share all these attitudes, but more representative of their leaders is an attitude of serious concern. It is true that they tend to regard alarm over absolute overpopulation as maneuvering on the part of propagandists who are eager to promote a pet theory of control by a fast sale. But on the question of relative overpopulation, they are ready for an all-out effort. They want to see every proposed solution scrutinized without emotion and every proper advantage taken of it. Each one presented so far seems incomplete, but taken altogether they are impressive and to a degree reassuring.

These solutions fall roughly into two classifications. Some are directed toward increasing the supplies, some toward decreasing the consumers. The first group seeks greater production, wider distribution, freer immigration, and stricter conservation. The second group centers on retarding the growth of the population.

With regard to the first group, there is no official attitude on the part of the Roman Catholic Church except one of deep interest, prompted by charity and a sense of justice, in alleviating hunger and misery wherever they exist. Pope Pius XII frequently emphasized the fact that the earth's resources were created for all men, so that where real need exists, a surplus must be shared with the destitute. Otherwise the various proposals of science arouse various degrees of enthusiasm in various quarters. One group is all for greater land use. Instead of cultivating only 7 percent to 10 percent, they point out that we could be raising crops on 52 percent. A second group is fascinated by the possibilities of the sea. Salt water can now be made sweet and used to irrigate the deserts, while rich sources of food in marine life are almost unexplored.

With others, the emphasis is on methods. Want would be sharply reduced if India would learn from the Japanese, and the whole world from the Dutch; if the agricultural mechanization of the United States could become universal; if cattle breeding were better understood, storage more efficient, and insects under better control. And so it goes. With the amazing advances of scientific research, new possibilities of increased production are coming to light every day, while the same can be said of distribution and conservation. Each item considered by itself may be an incomplete solution, but if all were even partially developed and existing surplus distributed with a little wisdom, the situation could be greatly improved in the danger spots of the world, relieving what we call relative overpopulation. With regard to all this great area then, there is no point of view peculiar to the Roman Catholic Church.

What then of the second classification, of the solutions aimed at retarding the increase of population? Here moral questions assume a greater prominence. We are dealing with human conduct, and among Catholics principles which are essential in determining right from wrong receive unanimous acceptance. Like old-fashioned Protestants and Jews, Catholics recognize the existence of the absolute, the existence, that is, of values that are eternal. Despite the customs of a particular generation, or a majority vote in a fallible legislature, some things are intrinsically evil and can be recognized as such by human reason. We are convinced moreover that a desirable purpose cannot justify an intrinsically evil action, or, in the more familiar phrase, that the end never justifies the means. So while we may all agree that relative overpopulation should be avoided, we may differ seriously with regard to the way in which this worthy result is to be achieved.

If efficiency were the only norm to be used in our selection, we should probably be forced to take the least defensible means. Since the primary occasion of population pressure is a fall in the death rate, the simplest plan to relieve the pressure would be to increase the death rate. After all, the easiest way to eliminate hunger is to eliminate the hungry. Once the Divine Law has been put aside, this can be done by several recognized methods. One we learned from Hitler. His "ultimate solution of the Jewish problem" could be tried out on the beggars of India. Another has become famous by its success in Soviet Russia and China. In both places, unknown millions of mouths, some hungry, some merely loud, have been taken care of with triumphant efficiency. More suitable, however, to our tastes—the Americans and British are so sentimental about these things—would be the adoption of wholesale euthanasia, which could eliminate the helpless, the unemployable, the backward, the difficult, the sick, and all those who are poor and over sixty. Given a generous interpretation, it could include half the population of the world. Easier to introduce because public opinion is so well prepared, would be the legalized murder of unborn children. The only objection is that it seems illogical to sacrifice possible leaders of the future, when euthanasia can select for painless elimination those whose future is behind them. Of course, mass sterilization would create much less of a mess and would be almost as satisfactory, if it could be easily enforced and the world could afford to wait for results. Contraception, most ardently advocated among the privileged nations at the present time, is the least efficient where it is thought to be needed most. The undesirable peoples who are being encouraged to regulate their numbers, will not take the trouble to learn or observe the necessary procedures, and a billion have to be indoctrinated right away at enormous expense. They are superstitious or ignorant or lazy or, in many cases, go so far as to love having little babies of their own. If they washed more frequently, they might be mistaken for conservatives.

With regard to all these systems of reducing the population pressure, there is a wide difference of opinion. But each one has its own champions today in popular, scientific, and religious circles. Condemning them all as immoral, not merely as forbidden but as intrinsically evil means that cannot be used to bring about even a good and necessary end, the Catholic Church is far from alone, though support from outside opinion gets weaker as we go down the list. Wholesale massacre, whether by gas or government-induced famine, would find little public support at present in most parts of the world. Euthanasia has the advantage of an organized body of enthusiasts, though the more mature among them are said to be giving trouble. They show a tendency to extend the age limit. Legalized abortion is publicly advocated by letters in national magazines and millions wince when it is referred to as murder. Many would welcome mass sterilization if they could select for experimentation the particular race they find most uncongenial. But on the question of contraception, the Catholic Church, while not yet alone, is certainly more conspicuous than she used to be. She does not accuse all those who disagree with her of high crimes and misdemeanors. She realizes that many excellent people do not grasp the implications of this practice as their parents did, do not as a matter of fact believe any longer in the existence of the Natural Law. Many of our intellectual leaders have not taken it seriously since it was banished from the United States Supreme Court by Oliver Wendell Holmes and vanished subsequently from most of our best law schools. But the old Church has always distinguished between morality and legality, between sin and crime. It has to keep on condemning contraception, not because some Pope or Council forbade it, but because she still sees it as a violation of the Natural Law, as a perversion of right order which destroys the meaningfulness of the marriage act and creates as many difficulties as it seeks to avoid, whether moral, physical, psychological, or merely aesthetic.

Does that mean that the Catholic Church and the non-Catholics who still agree with it, are entirely negative with regard to birth control? By no means. They all rejoice when birth is controlled by the elimination of early marriage, polygamy, concubinage, fornication, and adultery. Furthermore, many join the Catholic Church in following St. Paul who said of the unmarried that "it is good for them so to continue, even as I." As a consequence, there are in the United States alone, at least 235,000 celibates among its priests, nuns, and brothers, not to speak of seminarians and the laity. Even among married couples it is formally acknowledged that there are often good reasons for the spacing of the expected children and that this sort of birth control can be achieved without violating the Natural Law, by the practice of periodic continence. While admitting that periodic continence is difficult, the

Church refuses to admit that it is impossible for those who are making an honest effort at union with God.

To sum it all up then, when the Roman Catholic Church discusses population pressure, its proximate interest is in relative overpopulation, and in this area, even its leaders are not unanimous on all details, but only on general principles. They recognize the gravity of the present situation and its connection with a possible World War, though they remain on their guard against the exaggerations of propagandists. They are convinced that charity and justice in sharing surplus foods and the benefit of education, should go hand in hand with every practical variety of scientific development which may improve production, distribution, and conservation. But since there are evils worse than malnutrition and the end can never justify the means, all those who still share the ideals of the Catholic Church would limit their solutions in the present crisis to those which they recognize as conforming at least with the Natural Law.

THE RT. REV. JAMES A. PIKE, Bishop of the Episcopal Diocese of California, received his A.B. and LL.B. degrees from the University of Southern California in 1934 and in 1936, a J.S.D. from Yale in 1938, and a B.D. from Union Theological Seminary in 1951. He is a member of many professional, civic, and religious organizations, and an officer, past or present, in several of them: The National Urban League (director; chairman, Housing Commission, New York City), American Academy of Political and Social Science, Council for Middle Eastern Affairs, National Council of Churches (delegate). He is the author of *Beyond Anxiety; Doing The Truth: A Summary of Christian Ethics; If You Marry Outside Your Faith; Next Day;* the co-author of *A Roman Catholic in the White House* and *Faith of the Church,* and editor of *Modern Canterbury Pilgrims.*

A Protestant's View

THE RT. REV. JAMES A. PIKE

The publication on July 14, 1961, of what may be one of the most important encyclicals in modern papal history, *Mater et Magistra,* served to sharpen again the differences which lie between Protestants and Roman Catholics in the area of concern over the population explosion. As part of the truly enlightened and generally acceptable consideration of the social problems facing the world today, and an imaginative attempt at their solution, Pope John XXIII has returned again to the traditional Roman Catholic position on artificial birth control and has stated flatly that such methods, insofar as the Roman Catholic Church is concerned, do not offer an acceptable solution to the population problem.

In so doing, Pope John has of course raised points with which Protestants would find themselves in hearty agreement. He points out, for instance, that there is more than one solution to the population-explosion problem, and that the earth may not yet be even within range of supporting the population it is capable of feeding and clothing. So far as I know, no Protestant would take the stand that birth control is the only solution, or that we should stop making efforts to take care of an expanding population, merely because it *could* be controlled by contraception if we so desire. Generally speaking, I think, the Protestant would hold an "across the board" view as to the solution of this problem, equally glad to see every possible method tried in meeting this tremendous challenge.

Elsewhere in this volume those who are experts in the subjects have dealt with the magnitude of the population explosion and with its meaning for our society. It is only fair to say that some of these views seem to be conflicting, and that it is quite possible for the churches to be confused as to precisely the nature of the demands made upon them. There are those who, in order to bolster the argument against the use of contraceptives, have actually stated that no population explosion exists, and that the very phrase is some kind of bugaboo dreamed up by the exponents of birth control in order to further their aim. This, it would seem to me, is not a responsible approach to the problem. We may differ as to the problem's extent, and even as to its immediacy, but surely nothing is served by refusing to look at it at all.

Both Protestants and Roman Catholics would agree, I am sure, that when any problem of serious magnitude faces the whole world, they are responsibly bound to contribute toward its solution. Roman Catholics are constrained, in attempting to make their contribution, by previous positions adopted, not in relation to the population explosion as such, but in relation to questions involving the individual family relationship. In some cases, Protestants are equally constrained, and by the same positions; but, by and large, as Protestantism has faced the new questions raised by the apparent nature of the population explosion, it has been able to reexamine previous convictions and, at least in some cases, to understand where these previous convictions were in error.

For many years Roman Catholics and most Protestants shared the view that the primary purpose of the sexual relationship was the procreation of children. According to this line of reasoning, any use of the sexual act which does not have at least the possibility of procreation within it is a perversion of that act. It is upon this premise that the present Roman Catholic position on contraception is built, as was the previous position of many Protestant groups.

However, in recent years, Protestants have been reexamining the nature of the sexual relationship, particularly in the light of sacramental theology, and many Protestant theologians are no longer able to accept the premise that procreation is the only primary function of the sex act. One sometimes hears the statement that there are at least two "primary functions"—which, of course, is only an ungrammatical way of saying that there is no *primary* function. According to this view, the sex act is a sacramental means of expressing love between a man and a woman, in which "the twain become one flesh." Under certain circumstances this act may result in procreation, but even if it does not, the sacramental nature of marriage has been expressed therein. A sacrament is an outward and visible sign of an inward and spiritual grace. The sex act can be this and like other sacramental actions is both "symbol" (in this case, of the inward love and commitment already there) and a "means of grace" (that is, a means of strengthening and "refueling" the binding love). It should be noted that this position differs markedly from that of those who say that the sex act has only the two functions of procreation and "pleasure"; for pleasure—simply as such —is essentially a selfish aim. Surely the relationship which is consummated in the sex act is far too deep and meaningful to be summed up in the word "pleasure." This would be, at least, the position of many Protestant theologians today.

With this premise as a starting point, the Protestant theologian then is able to consider those circumstances under which the act should or should not result in procreation. He is able to bring to bear upon this problem the whole range of the Christian doctrine of vocation, i.e., responsibility, and finally to declare that a married couple has a Christian responsibility in this area as in many others, namely, that of doing the will of God as they understand it. Thus, it would be perfectly proper for a couple to decide, before God, that they should at a given time make every effort to increase their family, and their so doing would be responsible behavior—and their failing to do so would be irresponsible. But by the same token it would be possible for them to decide that, because of circumstances beyond their control, or because of a real conviction as to God's will for them, they should *not* be increasing their family at a certain time; and then it would become incumbent upon them, not only permissibly but as a positive duty, to take such steps as are necessary to avoid having children. Some theologians would go even further, and say that given a couple who have decided that according to their best insights they should not be having children, this couple would then be guilty of positive irresponsibility if they did *not* use the best methods available to prevent conception. If they were convinced that artificial contraceptives represented for them the best method available, they would actually have a religious imperative to use these devices.

It is hard for one to speak of a "Protestant position," and it would be only honest to say that the "Protestant position" as it exists in the mid-twentieth century extends all the way from a position indistinguishable from that of the Roman Catholic Church, through the position stated immediately above, to one simply of "liberty"—which is not the same as the view of responsibility stated above. I do think it accurate to say, however, that the main stream of Protestant theological thought is in the direction herein indicated and is expressed in a recent statement of the National Council of Churches and in previous declarations of principal churches.

It should also be reemphasized that, so far as I am able to ascertain, no Protestant thinker on this subject feels bound by any one solution to the population problem. I myself have been active in proposals that the Federal Government join in research aimed toward making more effective the so-called "rhythm system" which is acceptable to Roman Catholics. All of the methods have in common the drawback that they are exceedingly difficult to teach to a backward population; and it may be that, if it could be made more accurate, the rhythm system would be easiest of all to bring into widespread use—and also would eliminate in our own country the political barriers in the way of technical assistance to overpopulated countries desiring our help.

By the same token, every effort must be made in the fields of economics, agronomy, etc., to make the world habitable for a greater population. Even were the entire population of the world to accept the necessity for artificial limitation of population, we are well on our way toward that "infinite explosion" which scientists tell us will occur early in the twenty-first century. In other words, we are all aware that an enlightened view on the use of contraceptives cannot do the job alone, and that we are merely wasting time when we debate with one another the relative merits of the different systems. All possibilities must be considered and probably all of them must be brought into play if the real danger is to be met with any sort of responsibility.

Protestants generally, too, have felt quite strongly the responsibility which accrues to mankind in bringing about a solution to this problem, since man has himself to thank for the problem in the first place. Even a few generations ago the whole concept of a "Population Explosion" would have been ridiculous, for we were so far from approaching the maximum number which the earth could support. However, with no thought that we were disturbing the "natural order," we have taken tremendous strides in what might be called "death control." We have increased the life span of people all around the world, we have succeeded in wiping out many of the most pressing problems which have beset us and which, to some extent, helped to control the population, and we have done these things in the name of mercy and concern for others. These things should have been done. There was no excuse for the average life-span, e.g., of the Indian, which was less than thirty years. But by changing this, we have contributed to the population problem. We must now attack it with the same single-mindedness and the same effectiveness that we used earlier upon such problems as famine and disease.

Finally, the problem is one which depends for its solution upon a far wider measure of education than has yet been allowed for. None of us wants to see the Orwellian state of *1984*, in which the government will be charged with telling each family how many children it can have. There will always be families without children and families with twelve or fourteen. However, as whole populations begin to see the problem for what it is, and begin to understand their responsibilities toward it, we may hope that an increased measure of responsibility will begin to make itself felt in various national birth rates. It may well be that some solution other than any we have thought of will present itself before the problem becomes finally critical, but the time is short; indeed, if our demographers can be trusted, it is running out. There is little more time for argument, and unless firm action is taken soon, it may well be too late to act at all.

PART V

Population Pressures on Morals and Ethics

Joseph Wood Krutch, drama critic, essayist, naturalist, and teacher, received advanced degrees from Columbia University (M.A. 1916, PH.D. 1923) and began teaching there in 1917. From 1943 he was Brander Mathews Professor of Dramatic Literature at Columbia. In 1950 he moved to Tucson, Arizona, to devote full time to writing. Dr. Krutch was drama critic for *The Nation* from 1924 to 1950 and is the author of many books on the theater, on eighteenth-century literature, and on nature. Among the last are: *The Desert Year, The Measure of Man, Grand Canyon,* and *The Forgotten Peninsula.*

A Naturalist Looks
at Overpopulation

JOSEPH WOOD KRUTCH

One of the many indications that the population explosion poses the most desperate problem of our day is the fact that it inevitably arises in connection with every approach to the analysis of our civilization and its prospects. To the critic of culture it is a part of our emphasis on quantity rather than quality. To the economist it raises the question of economic stability. To the political scientist it evokes the specter of wars for Lebensraum; to the conservationist the equally terrifying specter of universal starvation.

To the specialists in their various fields I leave the discussions appropriate to them and say only something about the situation as it appears to a naturalist; to one who is, of course, aware of its other aspects but tends to think first of man's place in nature and the consequences of modern man's refusal to accept the fact that he is indeed part of a scheme which he can to some extent modify but which he cannot supersede by a scheme of his own making.

It is true, of course, that man became man rather than simply a member of the animal kingdom when he ceased merely to accept and submit to the conditions of the natural world. But it is also true that for many thousands of years his resistance to the laws of animal nature and his modifications of his environment were so minor that they did not seriously interfere with natural law and required no such elaborate management of compensating adjustments as became necessary as soon as his intentions, desires, and will became effective enough to interfere with the scheme of nature.

It was not until well into the nineteenth century that his interferences did become extensive enough to force a dawning realization of the fact that you cannot "control nature" at one point without taking steps to readjust at another the balance which has been upset. Improved methods of agriculture exhaust the soil unless artificial steps are taken to conserve and renew it. You cannot destroy all the vermin without risking the destruction of useful animals. You cannot, as we are just discovering, poison noxious insects without risking the extinction of birds who are an even more effective control. It is not that we should not interfere with nature, but that we must face the consequences of this interference and counteract or ameliorate them by other interferences. You dare not, to put it as simply as possible, attempt to manage at one point and to let nature take her course at another.

Considered in connection with this fact the population explosion becomes merely a special (and especially ominous) example of a phenomenon characteristic of civilized

man's peculiar place in nature where he is the only creature capable of effectively interfering with her operations
while he remains at the same time not wise enough always
to foresee the unwanted consequences of his interference.
To reduce it again to the simplest possible terms, he has
interfered with nature by preserving individual lives far
more successfully than nature had ever been able to preserve them at the same time he has allowed nature to take
her course so far as propagation is concerned. As a consequence either one of two things must happen. Either he
must control birth as well as death or nature will step in
and by her own rough but effective methods—starvation,
disease, or the brutal death struggle for food and living
room—eliminate the excess which failure to manage the
consequences of his management has produced. No matter
what fantastic increases technology may bring in the number of men the earth is able to support, the limit must be
reached sooner or later.

Every ecologist knows that nature left to herself works
out a balance of populations adjusted to the available
space and food supply, and that this balance, which in-
volves the various aspects of competition including the
predator and his prey, is often remarkably stable over long
periods of time. But every ecologist knows also that it may
be disturbed and then destroyed by what might appear to
be the very slight intervention of man. Introduce and then
forget a few goats into the biota of an isolated island, and
in a few years nothing but goats—many of them starving
—will remain. Nature is efficient but slow. It takes centuries for her to work out a balance. Man can in a few
decades make a desert which nature cannot reclaim in
centuries. So it is also with instinct, which is geared to

millennia, while consciously directed purpose is effective within a few years. The instinct which tells us that the more children we can produce the better, developed in us when man was dominated by nature. It persists fatally in a world he has come to manage and mismanage.

Early proponents of planned parenthood assumed that once easy and reliable methods of birth control were available, convenient, and legal the only remaining impediment to a rational solution of the problem would be that of religious or moral resistance. But in my opinion the existence of the ancient instinct deep in the biological organism is a more formidable enemy than religious dogma. In the United States at least the population has been increasing at an accelerated rate at the same time that methods of birth control have become better known and more readily accessible. The only possible explanation is simply that people continue to *want* more children than is desirable now that the mortality rate has been so greatly reduced. Many who are intellectually convinced that population growth should be reduced nevertheless rejoice in at least their own large families because the impulse to increase and multiply was an instinct long before it was a biblical injunction. Man the thinker lags behind man the technician. No less important is the fact that his instincts lag, not years but millennia, behind even his thinking. The most crucial question is not can he be made to *believe* that too many children are undesirable, but can he conquer his instincts sufficiently to make him *feel* what his intellect has convinced him of?

So much for the special ways in which the naturalist sees the problem. He tends also to be more acutely aware than others of a particular aspect of the undesirable con-

sequences of overpopulation. Many sociologists and political scientists recognize the fact that the question is not
simply how many people the earth could possibly support, but what is the optimum number from the standpoint of the possibility of a good life. Just as it is foolish
to ask what is the largest number of children a family
could possibly consist of rather than how many constitute
an ideal family unit, so it is foolish to ask how many could
be crowded onto our globe rather than what number can
live happily there. Men need not only food and a place to
sleep but also room to move about in. It is at least possible
to believe that cities are already too big and that life
would become almost intolerable if they were both more
densely crowded and so merged one with another that
there was no escaping from them.

Of this the naturalist is often more acutely aware than
either the sociologist or the political scientist because he
is more completely convinced than they sometimes are
that the best life for the human being is one which is led,
partly at least, in the context of nature rather than in a
context which consists exclusively of the man-made environment. For a large part of the existing human race in
the centers of civilization, contact with the natural world
is tending to diminish almost to the vanishing point while
he has little experience with anything except bricks, steel
and concrete on the one hand and mechanical contriv-
ances on the other. As the cities spread and the country
shrinks he is more and more imprisoned with his fellows
in a world that has ceased to be even aware of many of the
things of which he was once an intimate part. Already he
has pushed into extinction many of the creatures with
which he once shared the earth.

Those who feel that he has already begun to suffer from this fact, talk about recreational areas, about nature education, about national parks and even about wilderness areas. To some extent they can still meet the objections of those who say that we cannot afford to forego the use of any of our forests, or mountains, or deserts. But if our population continues to grow at its present rate, it will soon become evident that we do indeed need every available acre of possibly usable land either for agriculture or for building lots. Much of what is called conservation today is no more than a useful delaying action. The time may soon come when it will no longer be possible to protest against the despoliation of this or that park, or forest, or river. Hence the conservationist also must face the fact that behind almost every problem of today lies the problem of population. Unless that problem is solved, none of the others can be.

Let us suppose for a moment that those are in the right who say that the context of nature has ceased to be the most desirable context for civilized life, that man can live in a wholly man-made world and that he will in time forget all that he once drew from his contemplation of that world of which he has ceased to be a part. Let us suppose further that his increase in numbers stopped before space itself gave out, and that he has reached what some seem to think of as the ideal state, i.e., living in cities which are almost coextensive with the surface of the earth, nourishing himself on products of laboratories rather than farms, and dealing only with either other men or the machines they have created.

What will he then have become? Will he not have become a creature whose whole being has ceased to resemble

Homo sapiens as we in our history have known him? He will have ceased to be consciously a part of that nature from which he sprang. He will no longer have, as he now does, the companionship of other creatures who share with him the mysterious privilege of being alive. The emotions which have inspired a large part of all our literature, music, and art will no longer be meaningful to him. No flower will suggest thoughts too deep for tears. No bird song will remind him of the kind of joy he no longer knows. Will the human race have then become men-like-gods, or only men-like-ants?

To this question the naturalist has his own answer just as he has his own answer to the question why population continues to grow so rapidly in a world already at least beginning to be aware that this growth is a threat. His approach may seem to others somewhat oblique, even distorted by his special interests. But at least his conclusions are the same as those to which many other approaches no less inevitably lead.

The Good Life

ANDRÉ MAUROIS

Translated by Lawrence G. Blochman

Until the outbreak of the First World War in 1914, we might have declared hopefully that mankind seemed to be making some progress toward civilization. The eighteenth century had been called "The Century of Enlightenment" and it is true that science, philosophy, and other matters of the spirit shone brightly during that period. Culture in the eighteenth century, however, was reserved for a numerically small elite; the masses remained steeped in superstition and fanaticism; torture and slavery had not been abolished. The nineteenth century and the beginning of the twentieth saw the rapid advance of democracy and justice. Manners had become gentler. A judicial error could arouse the whole world to indignation, as was seen at the time of the Dreyfus affair. Compassion, patience, and friendship among men seemed to be necessary virtues which the majority tried hard to practice.

In 1961, alas! we must record not further progress but a series of terrible retrogressions. During the course of the Second World War, we witnessed atrocities such as had not been committed for a very long time. Torture had become standard operating procedure rather than an exception lapse. Violence, either by war or mass disorders, had replaced negotiation and compromise. Political partisanship, nationalism, and racial hatred are today resorting to a terrorism that we had a right to believe was obsolete. Our very manners today are more brutal. Our films and our theater reflect a society in which noble sentiment is rare and a decent way of life held up to ridicule. Our screen is monopolized by murders, holdups, rapes, and orgies. As an indication of how far we have retreated from humanity, compare the motion pictures deriving from the daily life of our times with *La Princesse de Clèves*, a film based on a novel of the seventeenth century.

Why this retrogression? We might have expected the contrary. We might have hoped that democratic education, in giving everyone a chance to share the culture of the past, would have produced a more kindly society. It would seem that the knowledge of the humanities, that heritage common to all men, that vast religious, literary, and artistic patrimony which could unite all peoples in common admiration, should have rendered impossible a certain barbarism which we so aptly call "inhumanity." Actually, the humanities no longer exercise their benevolent influence. For the first time in history men have created the United Nations—and never before in history have men been so disunited. They have drawn up a Declaration of the Rights of Man applicable to all without discrimination because of country, race, or religion—and rarely have the rights of man been so widely disregarded in so many parts of the world. Why?

There are many possible answers to this question because there are underlying reasons of many different kinds which combine to produce the deplorable situation. There is of course the disastrous role played by the two great wars. There are the contributions of false doctrines and the philosophies of despair. And there is another cause, frequently overlooked, which I should like to underline here: *Overpopulation.* You may well ask: What relationship can there be between overpopulation and morals, between overpopulation and the humanities? I shall try to show that the relationship is very close indeed.

First of all, we must understand that the humanities, broadly speaking, are passed on from generation to generation through the media of the family and community. It is not by the philosophers that our children are taught good manners and morals; it is by example. In my biography of Adrienne de La Fayette, I described how girls were brought up in a religious family of the eighteenth century. There was no constraint; the mother appealed to her daughters' reason. But she was an admirable mother and nobody could possibly have lived with her without seeking to imitate her. The twelve-year-old of that time wrote letters which in the perfection of style and sentiment could be equaled by few people of our day, even the best and most intelligent.

Now, this familial education, as efficacious as it was solidly based, has disappeared almost entirely today. Our overpopulated cities consist of huge, hastily built barracks in which families that are too big, crowd into apartments that are too small. The children rarely stay home because there is no room for them to play. They go outside to play with the neighbors' children—perhaps to form the nucleus of one of the juvenile gangs which are becoming too nefarious in too many countries today. Education by example is out of style. The bond between generations has grown slack. If I may be permitted to cite a personal example, my own taste for letters was transmitted to me by my highly cultured mother who from my earliest childhood read to me from the great authors, adding her own commentary, so that I should get to know the masterworks of literature at first hand. Very few mothers today would have the chance to exert a similar influence on their offspring.

In the past, familial education was supplemented by community education. The village was a school of neighborliness and friendship. Because a villager knew all his neighbors and also knew that he was destined to spend his life among them, he strove to prove himself a man of good graces and good manners. But in our overpopulated world, the small community is becoming more and more scarce. In African and Asian countries, the law of the village and the law of the tribe have been the sources of all civilization. But since overpopulation and industrialization tend to create urban centers becoming ever more huge, what is to become of the ceremonies and good manners of the past? They are disappearing—or nearly. What has been the basis for our nobler sentiments? Love and affection, which thrive best in the smaller units of society. True, love is not dead, but in our day it assumes its most ephemeral and least lovely aspects. Sexuality will never replace tenderness, nor will it inspire either compassion or tolerance. It is rather akin to brutality.

The salvation of our civilization lies with the humanities as we may learn them from the great books. There is no finer school for fine sentiments than the great novels or the best of the theater. It should be the role of our universities to bring humanity back to its sources. If the universities throughout the world could teach men of all races that in our great poets and philosophers they have friends in common, a strong, invisible web would be woven to join all peoples. But in this domain, too, overpopulation exerts a sorry influence. Competition is bitter in an overpopulated world. Man once produced about as much food as he needed for himself. Today more people are crowded upon a land than the land can feed. Those in excess must learn to earn their living in another manner.

Unfortunately, they stand to earn a more generous living if they study subjects other than the humanities. The modern world, preoccupied especially with machines and armaments, demands engineers, pilots, physicists, chemists, doctors, mechanics. Education is daily becoming more scientific and more technical. If only the student had spare time enough to devote to the humanities! But the techniques of our age have become so complex that to master them a student has no time to spare. The peoples of Asia and Africa are all demanding technicians. The United States, the Soviet Union, the countries of western Europe must turn them out in growing numbers to meet the demand. As a result, the humanities are largely neglected today, and the qualities of style and precise vocabulary are declining in all countries. This creates a dangerous situation. Technicians capable of building powerful instruments of dreadful destruction are no longer able to understand the fine shades of meaning and the delicate distinction between words. They are therefore helpless to defend themselves against the cruel and absolute doctrines which turn their own techniques to the service of fanaticism.

An overpopulated earth will bring forth unintelligent generations because culture demands leisure and silence, which have become lost qualities. Our information media must drop their standards lower and lower in order to reach the level of the new masses, innumerable and unreasoningly exacting. An old Buddhist text predicts: "The time will come when grown men will have the intelligence of a child of ten. These ten-year-old men will be dominated by violent hates, violent malevolence, and a violent desire to kill." We are not far from the day when the murderous mechanism of the nuclear bomb will be placed at the disposition of leaders with infantile minds, leaders hard-pressed by starving multitudes. Should this day come, overpopulation will produce disintegration.

Can this movement be stopped? Can this tide be reversed? Without doubt, it can, but reversal will require great statesmen with the courage to stem the irrational increase of population throughout the world, to re-create within our great, swarming urban centers, the old civilizing cells—the family and the village, fountainheads of all culture, and to restore to favor in all their forms the humanities and the amenities of life. Is all this possible? The history of mankind does record examples of such great reversions. Christianity is one of them.

The wild proliferation of men is a cancer of our planet. A superficial cancer may be cured. But the cure requires treatment—and perseverance.

SIR JULIAN HUXLEY, author and biologist, is the grandson of T. H. Huxley, the great nineteenth-century biologist. He received his education at Eton and Balliol colleges, Oxford. Sir Julian taught zoology at Balliol and New colleges, Oxford, until 1925 when he became professor of zoology at King's College (London) and then in 1927 an honorary lecturer. In 1935 he resigned from his formal teaching position to devote full time to research and writing. He was Director-General of UNESCO from 1947 to 1948. Sir Julian received the Darwin Medal of the Royal Society (1957), the Darwin-Wallace Commemorative Medal of the Linnean Society (1958) and the Albert Lasker Award in Planned Parenthood (1959). Mr. Huxley is the author of many books on evolution and man's place in nature: *The Uniqueness of Man, Evolutionary Ethics, Man in the Modern World, Evolution and Ethics,* and *New Bottles for New Wine.*

Too Many People!

JULIAN HUXLEY

Overpopulation is the most serious threat to human happiness and progress in this very critical period in the history of the world. It is not so acute as the threat of atomic warfare, but is graver, since it springs from our own nature.

Thanks to the new vision which we have attained through the knowledge explosion, which has gone on parallel with the population explosion in the last half-century, we have a new vision of our destiny. We may say that today evolution in the person of man is becoming conscious of itself.

I do not want to amplify this at great length. I would remind you, however, that all reality is, in a perfectly genuine sense, evolution; that biological evolution on this planet has been going on for nearly three billion years, and that in the course of that period life has advanced (not only increased in variety, but advanced in organization) so that its highest forms, from submicroscopic pre-cellular units, became cellular, then multicellular, then through

223

hundreds of millions of years grew larger and more powerful with greater control over their environment and
greater independence of its changes, culminating in land
vertebrates and eventually in the latest dominant type,
now spread over the whole world—man.

And man is now, whether he likes it or not, and indeed
whether he knows it or not (but it is important that he is
beginning to know it), the sole agent for the evolutionary
process on earth. He is responsible for the future of this
planet.

Before we make up our minds what we ought to do in
the present crisis we must try to find what our ultimate
aim is as agent or guide of evolution.

Surely, it isn't just power. Surely, it isn't just to eat,
drink, and be merry, and say, "Well, what's posterity done
for us? To hell with posterity!" It isn't just mere quantity of
possessions or mere quantity of people. Nor is it just preparation for some rather shadowy after-life. I would assert
that it must be to conserve and to develop the resources
of the earth and the resources of our own nature. And
so our aim should be to increase the richness of life and
enhance its quality.

"Fulfillment" is probably the embracing word; more fulfillment and less frustration for more human beings
through greater realization of possibilities. We want more
varied and fuller achievement in human societies. We
want more variety and less drabness and monotony. We
want more enjoyment and less suffering. We want more
beauty and less ugliness. We want more adventure and
disciplined freedom, as against routine and slavishness.
We want more knowledge, more interest, more wonder,
as against ignorance and apathy. We want more sense of

participation in something enduring and in worthwhile projects, as against a series of competitive rat races, whether with the Russians or our neighbors on the next street.

In the most general terms, we want more transcendence of self in the fruitful development of personality. We want a greater flowering of human dignity and significance, not only as against human degradation, but as against further self-imprisonment in the human ego, and as against mere escapism.

Man has been overexploiting the natural resources of this planet. He has been misusing its soils and polluting its waters. He has wasted enormous amounts of resources which he ought to have conserved. Almost everywhere (though mainly in underdeveloped and overpopulated countries), more and more marginal land is being taken into cultivation, more forests are being cut down, more soil erosion is taking place. Everywhere (but in this case especially in the most "developed" countries) high-grade raw materials are being used up at a frightening rate, and lower-grade sources are having to be used. Almost everywhere the supplies of water are becoming insufficient. We are well on the way to ruining our habitat.

Furthermore, not content with destroying or squandering our material resources, we are beginning to destroy our resources of true enjoyment—spiritual, aesthetic, intellectual, emotional. We are spreading great masses of human habitation over the face of the land, neither cities nor suburbs nor towns nor villages, just a vast mass of urban sprawl or subtopia. And to escape from this, people are spilling out farther and farther into the wilder parts and so destroying them. And we are making our cities so big as to be monstrous. They are growing to an impossible size. Just as there is a maximum possible size for an efficient land animal—a land animal more than about twice as large as an elephant could not exist—so there is a maximum possible efficient size for a city. Cities like London, New York, and Tokyo have already got beyond that size.

Looking at the crisis more specifically, mankind is not only proliferating excessively, but increasingly so. In A.D. 1600 the total number of people in the world was only about half a billion. It first reached 1 billion at about the end of the nineteenth century. By 1950 it had passed 2 billion. Today it is 2¾ billion, and increasing by nearly 50 million a year. Every twenty-four hours it increases by over 140,000—the equivalent of a good-sized town; and every minute by about 100—the equivalent of ten baseball teams complete with coaches.

What is more, the *rate* of increase is itself increasing. Before the discovery of agriculture it must have been below one tenth of one percent per annum; it reached one percent only at the beginning of the present century, but by now stands at over 1½ percent, and is still going up.

Still worse, the increase is very unevenly distributed over the world. By far the highest increase is in the underdeveloped countries with the lowest standard of life, notably in Asia and Latin America. This is bad for several reasons. In the first place, it makes their development much more difficult. To develop an underdeveloped country to an industrial and social level where it can hold its own in the modern world and give its people a reasonable standard of life, needs a great deal of capital, technical skill, and trained manpower. If too many babies are born, too much of that capital and skill and manpower will be used up in providing food, housing, education, health, and other services for them, and will not be available for economic and technological development. Coale and Hoover, in their careful study of the problem, concluded that if India did not reduce its birth rate by about 50 percent in the next thirty-five or forty years it would never be able to break through from its state of underdevelopment and underemployment to a developed and developing industrially based economy; on the contrary, it would reach a point of no return, after which living standards would go down instead of up. And the same general conclusion applies to other countries, such as Pakistan or Indonesia, with a high density of population at a low economic standard of life.

Then there is, as everyone knows, a great gap between the average standard of life in developed and underdeveloped areas—between the haves and have-nots. Thus the average real income of the 200 million people of North America is nearly twenty-five times as high as that of the over 1600 million people of Asia, and the disparity in energy available to an inhabitant of the United States and of India is even higher. The existence of this huge gap produces jealousy and unrest, and has generated what has been called the Revolution of Expectation in the have-not countries—an expectation of aid which must at all costs be satisfied.

The bridging of this gap is linked with the population problem. To take the Indian example again, at the moment, though the production of food is just keeping up with the production of people, it will not be able to go on doing so unless the rate of population increase slows down.

Furthermore, a large proportion—about three quarters, according to the Food and Agriculture Organization—of the people in underdeveloped countries is undernourished—in plain words, not getting enough of the right food to eat—and increased food production must aim at satisfying this deficiency too. And about the same proportion is grossly undereducated—in plain words, illiterate. Finally, the economic gap is widening instead of narrowing—the rich countries are getting richer, the poor countries getting poorer.

Attempts to bridge the gap by aid and assistance to underdeveloped nations are eminently desirable, and indeed necessary, if we are to have a peaceful and prosperous world. However, as I have just pointed out, all the science and goodwill in the world cannot find a way of successfully industrializing a densely populated and underdeveloped country if its increase rate is too high.

In the long run the key to the problem is the reduction of the human birth rate. In the present century medical science, in conjunction with improved conditions of life, has markedly reduced the world death rate, but without any appreciable reduction in the birth rate. It has brought about what we may call "death control" on a world scale: the contemporary population explosion is the result. It is now necessary to supplement worldwide death control with worldwide birth control. Population control, by some form of birth control, is a prerequisite for anything that can be called progress or advance in human evolution, even in the immediate future. One major contribution that science can make is the discovery of better and simpler methods of birth control. The time has now come for the world and all its nations to think seriously about population policy.

When I say that we need a population policy, I do not mean that any national or international body is going to tell every woman how many children she may have, any more than the adoption of an economic policy will mean telling the individual businessman how much money he is allowed to make, and how he should set about it. Nationally it means that we recognize population as a major problem of national life, that we have a general aim in regard to it, and that we try to devise methods for realizing this aim. And the adoption of an international population policy does not mean dictating to underdeveloped countries or laying down the size of a nation's population. It means the recognition that population increase is a world problem, affecting every nation in many ways, and the determination to try to control it in the most helpful way. Among other things, it implies the right of the people of every nation to the best scientific information about birth control, and the duty of the UN, supported by the technologically developed nations, to carry out research on human reproduction and its control, and to provide the fullest information on the subject.

Already a few countries have an official or unofficial policy of population control—India, Pakistan, Fiji, Japan, Singapore, Barbados, Puerto Rico—but they need world encouragement and their policies should be integrated into a general and official world policy.

Public opinion is ready for this. In the last few years the barriers of prudery and religious opposition have been largely broken down, the population explosion has become news, and its resultant problems are widely discussed. But ideology, religion, and power politics are still inhibiting the UN in this matter. Owing to Roman Catholic pressure, the World Health Organization has not been allowed even to consider population density as a factor in world health. Roman Catholicism is barring the adoption of a birth-control policy in many countries, like those of Latin America, where it is most urgently needed, and is making it difficult for the United States and other Western powers to give open or effective support to birth-control measures. The USSR calls birth control Malthusianism and opposes it on ideological grounds. China has professed to regard the addition of 12 million to its population every year as a desirable source of strength (though I would prophesy that they will reverse their attitude within the next few years).[1] Many emergent African states seem to regard any suggestion of population control as a white man's trick designed to keep the black races down.

All I can do here is to make a few personal suggestions. In the first place, a group including both underdeveloped and developed nations—say, India and Pakistan (this is a subject on which they could and should cooperate), Norway and Australia—should introduce a resolution into the UN Assembly calling for concerted thought and action on world population. At the same time a resolution authorizing and requiring the World Health Organization to consider the effects of population density on health should of course also be introduced, the International Labor Organization should report on the effects of rapid population increase on employment, and UNESCO should be made to give serious thought to the impossibility of coping with

[1] There are signs that this is now taking place (March 1962).

world undereducation, of providing adequate classrooms, teachers, and textbooks for the education of the world's children, so long as too many children continue to be born.

This would imply some radical changes in assistance and aid programs. For one thing, scientifically advanced countries like those of North America and western Europe would be encouraged and expected to do much more research on birth-control programs on request. Then it is most important that every request for aid or technical assistance by an underdeveloped country should be considered in the light of its demographic situation, especially its rate of population increase. No grants or loans for development should be made unless the country was willing to frame and stand by a rational population policy aimed at limiting the growth of its population, and some of the aid would be allocated to help it implement any such policy. Otherwise, as I pointed out earlier, the aid is all too likely to be useless, washed down the drain of history by the flood of new babies: some grants may even be worse than useless, for, if their possible demographic effects on population growth are not taken into account at the time, they may provoke a new excess of multiplication. A commercial bank, if approached for a loan, has the right to ask for some guarantee of financial solvency from its clients. The World Bank and other loan-making and grant-giving agencies have not only the right but the duty to ask for some guarantee of demographic solvency from their national clients.

The essential point is that overpopulation is a world problem so serious as to override all other world problems, such as soil erosion, poverty, malnutrition, raw material shortages, illiteracy, even disarmament. The future of the whole human species is at stake. If nothing is done about it, in the next hundred years man will cease to have any claims to be the Lord of Creation or the controller of his own destiny, and will have become the cancer of his planet, uselessly devouring its resources and negating his own possibilities in a spate of overmultiplication. If we do nothing about overpopulation now, our children and grandchildren now living will have a much more difficult task when they grow up, as well as a much harder, more frustrated, and often more miserable existence.

The time is ripe for action. The population problem is being passionately discussed everywhere. To change the metaphor, it is waiting in the wings of the world's international stage, ready to come on into the central limelight. But who is to bring it onto that stage? The Iron Curtain countries still pretend that the problem does not exist, or even that it has been invented by bourgeois economists. The leading Western countries seem inhibited by overconservative caution and religious opposition. The first move is up to those nations which are suffering from too many people—underdeveloped but overpopulated countries like India, Egypt, the West Indies, Indonesia, Pakistan. Let them take concerted action to ensure that the population problem ceases to be regarded as an unmentionable and horrific specter, but is considered and dealt with frankly, scientifically, and practically in the center of the international stage. Let them continue to demand UN action. Let them insist that it is not only their problem, but a world problem.

Meanwhile, of course, let them give proof of their willingness to do all they can to cope with it themselves—let them arouse their own public opinion, integrate national birth-control campaigns within their health services, train doctors and village nurses in preparation for the campaigns, do research, launch pilot projects. And let them publicize their efforts and bring their plight to the notice of world opinion. Only so shall we get what is so necessary —a world population policy.

We must look at the question of population increase in the light of the new vision of human destiny which human science and learning has revealed to us. We must look at it in the light of the glorious possibilities that are still latent in man, not merely in the light of the obvious fact that the world could be made a little better than it is. We must also look at it in the light of the appalling possibilities for evil and misery that still remain for human life in the future.

I would say that this vision, of the possibilities of wonder and more fruitful fulfillment on the one hand as against frustration and increasing misery and regimentation on the other, are the twentieth-century equivalents of the traditional Christian view of salvation as against damnation. And I would indeed say that this new vision that we are gaining, the vision of evolutionary humanism, is essentially a religious one, and that we can and should devote ourselves with truly religious devotion to the cause of ensuring greater fulfillment for the human race in its future destiny. And this serious and concerted attack on the problem of population; for the control of population is, I am quite certain, a prerequisite for any radical improvement in the human lot.

SELECTED LIST OF READINGS

GENERAL

Bennett, Merrill K. *The World's Food; A Study of the Inter-relations of World Populations, National Diets, and Food Potentials.* New York: Harper & Brothers, 1954.

Brown, Harrison S. *The Challenge of Man's Future.* New York: The Viking Press, 1954.

——— *The Next Hundred Years: Man's Natural and Technological Resources.* New York: The Viking Press, 1957.

California Institute of Technology. *Resources of the World, A Speculative Projection.* Pasadena, California: California Institute of Technology, 1956.

Darwin, Sir Charles Galton. *The Next Million Years.* London: Rupert Hart-Davis, 1952.

Hawley, Amos H. *The Changing Shape of Metropolitan America: Deconcentration Since 1920.* Glencoe, Ill.: The Free Press of Glencoe, 1956.

Osborn, Fairfield. *The Limits of the Earth.* Boston: Little, Brown & Co., 1953.

Pickard, Jerome P. *Metropolitanization of the United States.* Washington, D.C.: Ruban Land Institute, 1959.

Piddington, R. A. *The Limits of Mankind: A Philosophy of Population.* Bristol, England: John Wright & Sons, 1956.

Stamp, Dudley. *Our Developing World.* London: Faber & Faber, 1960.

235

Vogt, William. *People! Challenge to Survival.* New York: William Sloane Associates, 1960.

Zimmerman, Anthony. *Catholic Viewpoint on Overpopulation.* Garden City, N.Y.: Doubleday & Company, 1961.

TECHNICAL

Bates, Marston. *The Prevalence Of People.* New York: Charles Scribner's Sons, 1955.

Belshaw, Horace. *Population Growth and Levels of Consumption, with Special Reference to Countries in Asia.* London: George Allen & Unwin, 1956.

Bogue, Donald J. *Applications of Demography: the Population Situation in the U.S. in 1975.* Oxford, Ohio: The Scripps Foundation, 1957.

Burch, Guy Irving and Pendell, Elmer. *Population Roads to Peace or War.* Washington, D.C.: Population Reference Bureau, 1945.

Carr-Saunders, Alexander M. *World Population: Past Growth and Present Trends.* Oxford, England: The Clarendon Press, 1936.

Chandrasekhar, Sripati. *Hungry People and Empty Lands: An Essay on Population Problems and International Tensions.* Boroda, India: Indian Institute for Population Studies, 1952.

—— *Population and Planned Parenthood in India.* London: George Allen & Unwin, 1955.

Cook, Robert C. *Human Fertility.* New York: William Sloane Associates, 1951.

Cragg, J. B. and Pirie, N. W. *The Numbers of Man and Animals.* London: Oliver & Boyd, 1955.

Davis, Kingsley, ed. "A Crowding Hemisphere: Population Change in the Americas." Whole issue, *The Annals of the American Academy of Political and Social Science,* Vol. 316, March 1958.

—— *The Population of India and Pakistan.* Princeton, N.J.: Princeton University Press, 1951.

—— "World Population in Transition." Whole issue, *The Annals of the American Academy of Political and Social Science,* Vol. 237, January 1945.

Demographic Yearbook. New York: United Nations, 1948 to present.

Dublin, Louis I. *The Facts of Life From Birth to Death.* New York: The Macmillan Company, 1951.

Francis, Roy G., ed. *The Population Ahead.* Minneapolis: University of Minnesota Press, 1958.

Glass, David Victor, ed. *Introduction to Malthus.* New York: John Wiley & Sons, 1953.

Hatt, Paul K., ed. *World Population and Future Resources.* Proceedings of the Second Centennial Academic Conference, March 1951. New York: American Book Company, 1952.

Hauser, Philip M., ed. *Population and World Politics.* Norman Wait Harris Memorial Foundation, 30th Institute, 1954, University of Chicago. Glencoe, Ill.: The Free Press of Glencoe, 1958.

—— *Population Perspectives.* New Brunswick, N.J.: Rutgers University Press, 1960.

Henshaw, Paul S. *Adaptive Human Fertility.* New York: McGraw-Hill Book Co., 1955.

Hertzler, Joyce O. *Crisis in World Population.* Lincoln: University of Nebraska Press, 1956.

International Population Conference, Vienna, 1959 (*Internationaler bevolkerungskongress,* Wien, 1959).

Kelly, George Anthony. *Overpopulation: A Catholic View.* New York: Paulist Press, 1960.

Landis, Paul H. *Population Problems: A Cultural Interpretation,* 2d ed. New York: American Book Company, 1954.

Landry, Adophe. *Traité de Démographie.* Paris: Payot, 1945.

Leibenstein, Harvey. *A Theory of Economic Demographic Development.* Princeton, N.J.: Princeton University Press, 1954.

Mair, George F., ed. *Studies In Population.* Proceedings of the Annual Meeting of the Population Association. Princeton, N.J.: Princeton University Press, 1949.

Malthus, Thomas Robert. *An Essay on Population.* London: J. M. Dent & Sons, 1933. 2 vols.

Meier, Richard. *Modern Science and the Human Fertility Problem.* New York: John Wiley & Sons, 1959.

Milbank Memorial Fund. *The Interrelations of Demographic, Economic and Social Problems in Selected Underdeveloped Areas.* New York: Milbank Memorial Fund, 1954.

Notestein, Frank W. *The Future Population of Europe and the Soviet Union.* Geneva: League of Nations, 1944.

Osborn, Frederick. *Population: An International Dilemma.* New York: Population Council, 1958.

Oser, Jacob. *Must Men Starve: The Malthusian Controversy.* London: Jonathan Cape, 1956.

Pearl, Raymond. *The Natural History of Population.* New York: Oxford University Press, 1939.

Political and Economic Planning. *World Population and Resources.* London: George Allen & Unwin, 1955.

"Population Control." Whole issue, *Law and Contemporary Problems,* Vol. 25, Summer 1960.

Russell, Sir Edward John. *World Population and World Food Supplies.* London: George Allen & Unwin, 1954.

Sax, Karl. *The Population Explosion.* New York: Foreign Policy Association, World Affairs Center, 1956.

——— *Standing Room Only: The Challenge of Overpopulation.* Boston: Beacon Press, 1955.

Smith, Kenneth. *The Malthusian Controversy.* London: Routledge & Kegan Paul, 1951.

Smith, T. Lynn. *Population Analysis.* New York: McGraw-Hill Book Co., 1948.

Spengler, Joseph J. and Duncan, Otis D., eds. *Population Theory and Policy: Selected Readings.* Glencoe, Ill.: The Free Press of Glencoe, 1956.

Sulloway, Alvah W. *Birth Control and Catholic Doctrine.* Boston: Beacon Press, 1959.

Taeuber, Conrad. *The Changing Population of the United States.* New York: John Wiley & Sons, 1958.

Taeuber, Irene. *Population of Japan.* Princeton, N.J.: Princeton University Press, 1958.

Thompson, Warren S. *Population Problems,* 4th ed. New York: McGraw-Hill Book Co., 1953.

———— *Plenty of People.* Lancaster, Pa.: Jaques Cattell Press, 1944.

———— *Population and Peace in the Pacific.* Chicago: University of Chicago Press, 1946.

United Nations, Department of Economic and Social Affairs. *The Future Growth of World Population.* New York: United Nations, 1958.

———— *Population Studies.* Studies on various countries. New York: United Nations, 1948 to present.

United States National Resources Committee, Science Committee. *The Problems of a Changing Population.* Washington: U. S. Government Printing Office, 1938.

Whelpton, Pascal K. *Needed Population Research.* Lancaster, Pa.: Science Press, 1938.

World Population Conference, Rome, 1954. *Proceedings,* 6 vols., and *Summary Report.* New York: United Nations, 1955.

Woytinsky, Wladimir S. *World Population and Production: Trends and Outlook.* New York: The Twentieth Century Fund, 1953.

BIBLIOGRAPHY

Eldridge, Hope T. *Materials of Demography.* New York: Columbia University Press, 1959. Published for The International Union for the Scientific Study of Population and The Population Association of America.

JOURNALS

American Eugenics Society. *Eugenics Quarterly,* Vol. 1, No. 1, March 1954—to present.

Eugenics Society (London). *Eugenics Review,* Vol. 1, 1909— to present.

Indian Institute for Population Studies. *Population Review,* Vol. 1, No. 1, January 1957—to present.

International Union for the Scientific Study of Population. *Le Démographe,* No. 1, April 1955—to present.

Milbank Memorial Fund. *Quarterly,* Vol. 1, 1923—to present.

Office of Population Research, and Population Association of America. *Population Index,* Vol. 1, No. 1, 1935—to present.

Population Investigation Committee. *Population Studies,* Vol. 1, No. 1, June 1947—to present.

Population Reference Bureau. *Population Bulletin,* Vol. 1, No. 1, 1945—to present.

United Nations, Department of Social Affairs, Population Division. *Population Bulletin,* No. 1, Dec. 1951—to present.